Customer
═══════ with a
Capital C

Customer

with a

Capital C

Customer-Centric Service in a Nutshell

Ken Welsh

PARTRIDGE

A Penguin Random House Company

Other Books by Ken Welsh
Happy About Customer Service?
Who Killed Customer Care?

To order additional copies of this book, contact
Toll Free 800 101 2657 (Singapore)
Toll Free 1 800 81 7340 (Malaysia)
orders.singapore@partridgepublishing.com

www.partridgepublishing.com/singapore

This book is dedicated to anyone who has ever dealt with someone who left them thinking *I wish I had been treated like a human being. I know I treat my Customers better than that. ... Don't I?*

It is also especially dedicated to the team at Headsets.com for genuinely caring about their Customers, treating them as real human beings and including me as part of the Headsets.com family.

Plus, let's be realistic: without my amazing mother, Marcia, fantastic father, Don (also my best mate- yes I'm an Aussie so I still use the word *mate)* and Francesca, my super-supportive and tolerant partner of twenty-plus years, this book could never have happened.

Then, of course, there's the team at *Leichhardt*, especially Peter, Clare, Ellie and Chris, who helped balance my work and life enough to make this book possible.

Contents

A Message with a Capital *Mmmm?*

Thank you for joining me on my personal adventure in Customer Service.

It all started when I met Mike Faith, founder of Headsets.com and a self-professed Customer Service Fanatic.

Mike changed my life, and I hope through reading this book and sharing my adventure I can change yours.

Along the way, I'd like you to keep this in mind:

A journey is your movement from A to E, via B, C, and D.
An adventure is something unexpected
that happens to you along the way.

Enjoy your adventure!

Ken Welsh
www.kenwelsh.com

Acknowledgments

This book could never have been written without the incredible dedication of Mike Faith and his team at Headsets.com. I could easily fill three pages with acknowledgments to everyone that has worked with me in this amazing company, and of course to the company's incredible Customers and suppliers.

Everyone at Headsets.com has been endlessly supportive of my work and has tried out my ideas, modified them, and helped them to evolve into, what I like to think is, the world's best Customer Experience package.

In particular, I'd like to thank the following people:

- Mike Faith, for his endless support and for being my champion and friend for many years, and also for his vision (without which I would never have experienced Customer Service as it really should be);
- Jordan, for running an amazing team in San Francisco;
- Kevin with his incredible team in Nashville;
- Anne-Marie, Shandi and Marty for their brilliant training regime at Headsets.com;
- Art and Jenny, an amazing credit control team;
- Lawrence, Bren, Shelby, Cindi, Stephanie, Bryan, Ryan, Jena, Peter, Steve, Kayla, Troy, Jeff, Josh, Brett, Ashley, Rebecca, Annie, Anita, Caitlyn, J'Allen, Jack,

Heidi, Susie, Matt, Leslie, JD, Corey, Ethan, Dave, Leah, Cassandra, Didi, Gordon, Courtney, Amber, Phil, Ronnie, Jacob, Jake, Matthew, Horacio, Chris, Mike (yes there's a few), - generally the team old and new (clearly I can't name everyone individually) so basically every person who works or has worked with Headsets.com.

To you, my dearest friends, thank you all.

Introduction

The Purpose of This Book

First,

I'd like to make it very clear that while this book is about Headsets.com, a company that I have coached for over a decade, it is not meant to be an advertisement for that company. I was not paid to write this book for Headsets.com. In fact, *I asked them* if I could write about them, because I genuinely feel that they set a benchmark in world-class Customer Service for medium-size companies.

If you have a small family business, it's relatively easy to give great Customer Service, because you pretty much know all your Customers personally, and they you. If you're a massive Customer-focused multinational with bucket loads of money to throw at publicity, rewards, and promotion, you can pay for your people to give great service, and you can also more or less convince people that they have received great Customer Service even if they haven't. You can virtually *buy* a Customer's loyalty.

It's the companies in the middle that can find it challenging.

That said, let's talk about this book.

In our modern world, as economies ebb and flow and competition for Customers becomes increasingly global,

Customer Service has become the great differentiator for consumer choice. If Customers are permitted to choose between several companies providing similar products at similar prices, they'll normally choose the company that treats them the best.

In my opinion, the company that this book focuses on, Headsets.com, consistently provides world-class Customer Service and sets a benchmark for other companies to aspire to—basically, they treat their Customers best. In fact, several of the Headsets.com team members that I coached have since moved on to establish Customer Service Excellence Teams with some of North America's premier companies.

This book has been written as a how-to guide using the model that was developed at Headsets.com over the past ten years. While I've been their voice coach for the past decade, their unique approach to the Customer Experience has grown out of ideas contributed by everyone in the company. In my work as a voice coach, I don't simply work on how people sound. I work with the overall package: the tone, rhythm, words, message, delivery, and reception as well as the context and psychological impact of what they say and how they say it. However, this is merely part of the Headsets.com experience.

By applying the Customer Service standards and concepts that Headsets.com has developed over the past ten years and adapting them to your type of business, you too can become the best Customer Service provider in your industry. It's that simple.

To help you remember the key elements of this book and how they can help you, I've included a brief do-it-yourself box at the end of each chapter, where I invite you to write down your thoughts and ideas.

And you're more—much more—than welcome to email me at ken@kenwelsh.com to tell me how you've taken your Customer Service to amazing new levels.

An Extra Note

Since I started writing this book, the world has changed and continues to do so. Headsets.com established its second base in Nashville, new team members have been introduced to its techniques, and some team members have moved on and introduced elements of the Headsets.com culture elsewhere.

Although a few names and places have changed, the principles still stand strong. So enjoy reading, learning, using, adapting, and evolving them.

So let's get to it .... Enjoy!

CHAPTER 1

Customer with a Capital C: What's This All About?

In a world where people have become mere numbers and the Customer Service dial is often broken—stuck on a very low level—a few companies still strive to make Customers feel special.

Many companies justify their low quality of service delivery by saying it is a cost-cutting measure in a highly competitive economic environment.

Really! How far from the mark can they be?

High-quality Customer Service is one of the most cost-effective Customer-development and retention tools we have available to us.

By applying a series of simple, low-cost techniques (for example, knowing the right words to say at the right time and the right way to say them), we can ensure that our Customers:

- remember us,
- choose us to buy from when they are ready to buy,
- come back to us to buy more, and

- tell other people about us—and encourage them to buy from us.

What more could you want?

That's what this book is about: helping you to create a unique and positive feeling in your Customers consistently so they want to deal with you—and only you—time and time again. Throughout this book, we'll explore ways that a moderate-size company has managed to do this for nearly a decade with a moderate capital outlay.

We all know the Big Five in Customer Service: Virgin, Nordstrom, Singapore Airlines, Emirates, and Ritz-Carlton. And yes, we all know that they have substantial capital behind them to ensure that they get things right.

I've flown on Virgin and bought CDs and DVDs in its stores, shopped at Nordstrom, experienced amazing in-flight service with Singapore Airlines, been the recipient of Emirates Airlines' famed luxury, and stayed at a Ritz-Carlton. I've experienced a gratifyingly high level of comfort, convenience, and service with all of them. Each of them has its own unique style and approach to Customer Service.

Ritz-Carlton, Nordstrom, and Emirates clearly push the envelope on luxury, and I admit I find it easy to feel satisfied when I'm sitting in a sumptuous hotel room while looking at magnificent city views, relishing comprehensive 24/7 room service. In comparison, the Virgin Group has chosen a slightly different, however still very successful, route to Customer Service Excellence: fun!

Now, while I do love luxuries, as most of us do, they come at a price—a price that not all of us can afford all the time. I guess that's why they're called luxuries. I also know that I love enjoying myself, so if my Customer Experience is enjoyable, easy, and affordable, I'll keep coming back.

It's a bit like love. Some of us are fortunate enough to fall in love with rich people. That means we can have fun and luxuries; however, in many places, there just aren't enough rich people to go around, so we fall in love with someone else. And that someone else is usually someone we enjoy being with. I am pretty happy with that process. I do like luxuries, however I really love a good laugh, and if I had a choice of one or the other, I'd go with enjoyment anytime.

So back to the Virgin experience. Virgin uses a combination of fun, efficiency, professionalism, and simplicity, and it encourages each of its associated companies to create its own unique ratio of the mix.

- Virgin Megastores capitalizes on friendliness, youth, and vitality; gives its frequent shoppers a VIP (Virgin Important Person) card; and addresses Customers by name whenever possible.

- Virgin Australia was originally a low-cost carrier that has redefined itself several times to create a niche that includes many business services, a business lounge, premium seating areas, and a frequent flyer program (Velocity). It also publishes its on-time performance on its website. Virgin Australia uses friendliness and fun combined with professional efficiency to captivate its guests. For example, the cabin crew uses the term *guest* rather than *passenger,* and you are addressed by your first name when you are directed to your seat.

- Virgin Mobile UK is a cell phone company that combines youth and enthusiasm with positive language and a simple, clean approach to business, making life easy for its Customers. So much so that it has won Best Customer Service at the Mobile Choice Consumer Awards for seven consecutive years.

With two hundred Virgin-branded companies employing fifty thousand people in twenty-nine countries and with a 2006 worldwide revenue in excess of $20 billion, it's clear that the Virgin formulae (in all of their various permutations) is successful.

Yet being a mega-company with massive financial resources doesn't guarantee great Customer Service, even if you throw bucket loads of money at it. Likewise, small businesses are by no means excluded from Customer Service Excellence. In many ways, small family businesses—such as small hotels and corner stores—can find it much easier to serve their Customers well. They have a small number of staff, so they can train and monitor them easily, and they have a relatively small clientele, which permits them to know them personally so they can cater to their unique needs.

This means that medium-size businesses often find Customer Service the most challenging. They regularly suffer from what I refer to as Gangly Teenager Syndrome. This is when a small company has grown rapidly, a little like your average adolescent, who starts to lose coordination as his arms and legs become a bit longer than he's used to, and he hasn't had enough experience to adapt. I distinctly remember how frustrated my father, a well-known local athlete, would become when he threw or hit a ball to me, his teenage son, and my left hand didn't know what my right hand was doing. The ball would either whiz by me or hit me in the head. Ouch!

It took hours of practice for me to hit, kick, and catch a ball. While I still am not an elite athlete, I can hold my own through wisdom gained by experience, and I haven't lost the enthusiasm of my youth.

Many medium-size companies have a mix of old and new

- Customers,
- staff,
- management,
- technology and equipment, and
- training.

This mix can result in an internal culture and external Customer Service that are inconsistent, to say the least.

Many moderate-size businesses stagger through their growth periods either blissfully unaware of what they could be achieving or hoping that one day it will all fall into place. These companies will benefit most from the contents of this book, although the principles that follow can benefit everyone.

How? Why?

In my opinion, the benchmark for the World's Best Practice in Customer Service Award is being set by a moderate-size San

Francisco– and now Nashville–based company that simply sells telephone headsets: Headsets.com. A key element of its approach to Customer Service is that it doesn't sell headsets; it helps its Customers buy headsets. And, most importantly; Customers are so important that they are always referred to with a capital C. That is, they're important enough to be a proper noun. They are as important as any big name, town, or country, because without their Customers, Headsets.com would not exist.

This capitalization is a key element in the Headsets.com version of Customer Service. Or as Headsets.com calls it, "Customer Love." Customer Love, the Headsets.com way, isn't simply great service; it includes every aspect of helping Customers and making them feel good, even if it doesn't seem to be in the short-term interest of the company. Headsets.com has its sights set on the big picture, the long-term goal of enduring Customer loyalty.

While some companies use some aspects of Headsets.com's Customer Service style, it is the result of the unique way in which its unique team puts its unique combination into practice. I'm sure you have already concluded that I feel Headsets.com is—you guessed it—unique.

Right up front, I declare my bias. I have coached Headsets.com for ten years and have proudly watched it become the best at what it does: treat its Customers as real people. It's as simple as that. Genuinely put yourself in your Customers' place, and you'll always create an incredible Customer Experience.

I know that many companies claim to deliver great Customer Service; however, Headsets.com has taken Customer Service, moved it through Customer care, and created Customer Love.

Everyone at Headsets.com knows about Customer Love. It's more than Customer Service, more than creating satisfied Customers. In fact, at Headsets.com, if you only satisfy your Customer, you clearly haven't done enough.

Every member of its team actively pursues service excellence, with every call it takes and every conversation it has. Yet it's more than that. It's more than simply when it's dealing one-on-one with its Customers.

You'll start to see what I mean as we look at some of the differences between Headsets.com and the Big Five mentioned earlier.

Every day that I'm in Headsets.com's Customer Contact Center, I hear dozens of Customers asking for product support for a headset that—they'd hesitantly explain—they don't think they bought from Headsets.com. When this is said, there's not a moment's delay as the "Customer Love expert" replies, "That's perfectly all right. I can definitely still help you. Let me set up a product support ticket for you so you'll have free lifetime product support from us any time you need it."

I've also heard members of the Headsets.com team help a Customer buy something from someone else. Yes, they'll refer a Customer to another company rather than sell a product that isn't the best possible fit for that Customer's specific needs.

Now, that's a bit like asking Emirates to honor a ticket for JetBlue, or Ritz-Carlton to honor a reservation you've paid Super 8 for, or to buy something from Nordstorm using a Radio Shack gift voucher. I've never had the temerity to make a request like one of those; however I can clearly imagine the response I'd likely receive.

The language everyone at Headsets.com uses is the most positive I have ever experienced. It is company-wide, from the technical support team to the Customer Love experts to the CEO. Everyone is uniformly held accountable for using his or her brand of positive language.

If you spend any time at all in the company's two contact centers (San Francisco and Nashville), you will be amazed at the complete buy-in to the power of positive language. Words like *can't, won't, don't,* and *but* are non-existent in the Headsets.com vocabulary.

This by no means detracts from the amazing service cultures developed by major players like Singapore Airlines, Burj Al Arab Hotel, and exclusive boutique hotels, such as Nukubati Island Resort in Fiji. I have no doubt that they genuinely care about their Customers. Again, size is not the determining factor; it is easy for a family that owns a bed and breakfast to excel at Customer Service, because they answer to no one, and their livelihood depends on word of mouth and referrals. And a cash-rich multinational can spend a small fortune to ensure its Customers' needs are catered for.

Small to medium-size businesses constitute the majority of businesses in the world, and many of them tend to be so focused on staying viable day-to-day that they miss the long-term advantage of the goodwill established and nurtured through Customer Service Excellence.

Headsets.com is my favorite example of what can be done when a medium-size enterprise has the vision, will, and perseverance to create and maintain a comprehensive Customer Service Package—the most thorough I have had the pleasure to experience.

Here we're not talking about a company with a bottomless pit of capital resources; we're talking about a company that started with forty thousand dollars of the CEO's own money. Money clearly wasn't the catalyst; vision and persistence were.

Anyway, back to the main point of this story.

We all know people, or even companies, that use positive language. They always smile while on the phone and thank their Customers for calling. It's pretty much becoming the norm. But something that makes Headsets.com special, perhaps even unique, is the team's unanimous buy-in to having a comprehensive skill set that places the total Customer Experience above all else.

In ten years, Headsets.com has moved from being a simple headset discounter to a leader in its field, with numerous awards to show for it. Even more importantly to the Headsets team are literally dozens of folders of Customer fan mail on display. There are over 320,000 pieces of such mail—and counting.

Headsets.com has reinvented Customer Service as Customer Love (and naturally enough, it comes with a capital C and a capital L), and I have been fortunate to be included in their journey to achieving world-class Customer Service.

After a decade working with the Headsets.com, coaching their teams, listening to and talking with their Customers, and bouncing ideas around with their trainers, marketers, and mentors, I'm convinced that every Customer really does deserve to be a

Customer with a capital C.

Your First "What Will I Do?" Box

In this first box I'd like you to answer a few questions. Future boxes will require you to make three commitments to action. Then it's up to you to follow through with them.

a) What do we want to achieve in Customer Service?

....

....

....

....

....

b) How do we want to be remembered by our Customers?

....

....

....

....

....

c) What are our current Customer Service strengths?

....

....

....

....

....

CHAPTER 2

Faith with a Capital M
(for Mike)

I n the beginning, yes, even before I came along, a few members of the current Headsets.com team were working with Mike Faith on one of his early entrepreneurial enterprises, a company called Office Timesavers. Prior to this, Mike, an Englishman from Southampton, had been known as a serial entrepreneur.

Mike was renowned for his rapid-fire ideas. Some of his longtime friends told me that he had a twenty-a-day habit. Ideas, that is!

Office Timesavers developed the Code Tracker, a simple concept with a nationwide market. The Code Tracker is a small map of the United States that includes the main telephone area code under the name of each state and a table of cities with their area codes on the reverse.

The Code Tracker proved relatively successful and to this day is on the workstations of every Headsets.com employee and is often included as a free gift for special Customers. I was given one on my first day at Headsets.com, and I'm still using it.

Along with Office Timesavers, Mike and his team ran National Legal Posters and a boutique travel book company—all of them from one office space.

Mike was never one to stay still for very long. It was a case of the more ideas the merrier, so the repertoire of projects steadily grew. Some were successful, some not quite so.

Of course to keep all of these irons in the fire, Mike was always busy, on the phone, writing things down, talking, typing—everything at once.

He's not the type of person to do one thing at a time. In order to do all these things at once, he used a telephone headset. This gave him the ability to talk, type, sketch, and even mute his telephone conversation when he needed to say something to someone else. He could do all of this without stifling his boundless energy by getting a stiff neck from cradling a telephone handset on his shoulder for hours at a time.

Mike loved his headset. And it dawned on him (probably idea number seventeen or eighteen for the day) that other people would love them too. He wanted to share his love and— never one to miss an opportunity—he knew there would probably be a profit in it as well.

The original headset sales company was born (not Headsets. com, a discounter designed to sell as many headsets as quickly and cheaply possible). Suddenly the Office Timesavers space became cramped as a team of temps took orders for telephone headsets. The company was on a roller-coaster ride with daily sales fluctuating significantly.

After a couple of years, the company hit a daily sales record: $19,000. This record sat unchallenged for quite some time.

In the meantime, Mike had become increasingly frustrated with the level of Customer Service that he'd been experiencing with other companies. In an average day, he was likely to deal with voice recognition systems or Customer Service reps who either couldn't speak English or knew next to nothing about their products—or worse, *both*. He thought; *Why can't people treat me the way they'd like to be treated if they were the Customer? I'd be prepared to deal exclusively with a company that treated me well, if only I could find one.*

The light bulb lit in Mike's head: "I can create that company!"

Soon Mike's team was to see that he was not only a twenty-ideas-a-day man (although he's the first to admit that he loves coming up with the ideas and then equally loves delegating them to someone else to make them happen), he was also a Customer Service Fanatic. This is a crown that Mike wears proudly.

Mike also speaks at conferences, seminars, and workshops as a Customer Service Fanatic, and his fanaticism is brandished across his personal website (www.mikefaith.com).

And so, Headsets.com was born, and the infant Customer Love was introduced to the world. Somehow, in his usual, passionate, persuasive, and infectious way Mike convinced his suppliers, his investors, and his team to come with him on his journey into the unknown.

This new company, Headsets.com, had a very demanding culture. It had a new approach to ... well, basically everything: talking with Customers, recruiting staff, the website, packaging, shipping, promoting, pricing, catalogues ... virtually anything that you could think of, and then some. Headsets.com was always trying something new.

Within a year, Headsets.com was building its reputation for Customer Service Excellence and bringing in a reliable, respectable annual revenue. A move to larger premises was made, and its purpose-built Customer Contact Center was created.

The seeds of Customer Love were well sown, watered, fertilized, and growing.

Price was no longer calling the shots; the company's performance standards were based on the results of Customer Service Surveys and how quickly Customer calls were answered. The company's approach was "sales will take care of themselves if we take care of our Customers."

What is now the ubiquitous Headsets.com Customer Service Excellence Ratio was soon established. To find out how their service was going, surveys were sent out with every headset sold, asking Customers to rate their experience with the company and the individual member of the team that they'd dealt with. The form had a simple 1–5 scale of poor, fair, good, very good, and excellent.

The team (and its individual members) wasn't rated on how good it was. Anything less than *excellent* on the survey was considered non-excellent, and that simply wasn't acceptable.

Their goal was to have an average of at least eight excellents for a single non-excellent.

This was pretty much a first at the time, and some team members who came from more traditional companies didn't always grasp the culture with both hands. There was definitely a period of adjustment.

Some people adapted, some left, and some new team members were recruited. It was a case of buy-in or leave.

Tough? Perhaps.

Worthwhile? Definitely!

About that time Mike tracked me down in Australia, and I started working over the phone with individual team members on the way that they sounded, the words they used, and the head space they needed to be in to achieve what was then considered an amazing goal: the 8:1 excellence rating.

Soon Headsets.com had established a reputation for amazing levels of Customer Service, and a loyal fan base of Customers developed—Customers who were much more than merely satisfied.

The validation of the success of Headsets.com's Customer Love is in the recognition that the company has received and continues to receive. The company's awards and commendations include the following:

- Fast 100: The Bay Area's Fastest Growing Companies (San Francisco Business Times): **2003, 2004, 2005, 2006, 2007**

- Finalist, Ernst & Young Entrepreneur of the Year®: **2004**

- Inc 500 Fastest Growing Companies: **2004, 2005, 2006**

- Best Places to Work as named by the *San Francisco Business Times, Silicon Valley/San Jose Business Journal,* and *East Bay Business Times*: **2005, 2006**

- Stevie® Award—4th Annual American Business Awards for Best Customer Service Team: **2006**

- Headsets.com CEO and President Mike Faith makes the Winning Workplaces Best Bosses list: **2006**

- Internet Retailer Top 500 List: **2007**

- Finalist Williams-Sonoma Emerging Growth Award, Excellence in Business Awards, SF Chamber of Commerce: **2007**

- Inc 5000 Fastest Growing Private Companies in the US: **2007**

Between 2001 and 2006, the company went from strength to strength, frequently breaking its own sales and Customer Service Excellence records.

During this period, the excellence target was raised from 8:1 to 9:1, then to 10:1, and excellence ratios were then introduced for product support, online Customer Service (live person/chat), and shipping. An overall excellence rating was also introduced for the Customer Contact Center as a whole, as well as for answer rates, maximum response times, and accuracy rates.

Then, of course, these standards were all raised as soon as it was proven that the team could maintain them. To this day, the practice of continually raising the bar is an intrinsic part of the company culture.

With the international economic downturn that began in 2007, sales figures leveled off, and staffing numbers stabilized. However, the company's Customer base and standards of service excellence continue to grow.

In the second quarter of 2009, while many companies were still tightening their belts and rationalizing their staffing, Headsets.com started recruiting again. Customer Support and support from Headsets.com's suppliers was so great that Mike successfully predicted an increase in demand (and additional Customer Service awards – which continue to roll in to this day).

Why? What gave the suppliers and investors confidence in this company when many others were still struggling for economic viability?

Customer Love—the Headsets.com Way

The feedback that the company was receiving from its Customers was that they would keep coming back (and observed behavior supports this). Why do they keep coming back?

Because they love being treated like the truly important people that they are. They know what they deserve, and they love being loved. They also love dealing with a company that values them enough to give them a capital C.

In addition to this, happy Customers readily share their experience with their friends and colleagues. They keep buying from Headsets.com, and they keep telling other people how great it is to buy headsets from Headsets.com.

What more could a company ask for?

What Will I Do to Change Our Approach?

Now you get to make your own suggestions. Fill in the spaces, then follow-through with your commitments.

a) Now—yes, right away!

....

....

....

....

....

b) By the end of this week

....

....

....

....

....

c) By the end of this month

....

....

....

....

....

CHAPTER 3

Thought with a Capital T

E very day each of us is a Customer in hundreds of ways, from when the alarm clock wakes us to when our local radio station announcer wishes us good morning to when our head hits the pillow at night.

Let's consider a typical day and how we were satisfied Customers even before our feet touched our bedroom floors in the morning.

For a start, if the power company had failed during the night, our clock wouldn't have work. Likewise, if the clock manufacturer hadn't made a product of a reasonable quality, it may not have woken us anyway. Our bed didn't let us down by collapsing during the night, nor did the blankets fall apart or give us a rash. So, things are looking pretty good for the day already.

We made our way to the kitchen. Our coffee is brewing, and the refrigerator has kept our milk fresh. Our cereal is still crunchy, the bowl has no cracks from faulty manufacturing, and our toaster browned the bread on both sides. Our clothes still fit, and our car started and even got us safely out of the driveway.

Up to this stage, we were satisfied, more or less. We'll probably continue to use the same clock until it dies. Then we may buy the same brand, even though it hasn't really done anything astounding for us. It's merely satisfied our needs at that time; we're more likely to buy the newest, best value clock when the time comes. *(Please forgive my occasional pun; you'll grow used to them—I promise.)* The same is likely to apply to the bed, the blankets, the toaster, coffee maker, the crockery, and even the breakfast cereal.

They've satisfied us—not necessarily pleased us, amazed us, or even captivated us. They've simply satisfied us, and we expect little more from items such as these.

We're on our way to work now. All is good—until we come to our regular morning traffic jam. In comparison to our toaster, clock, and cereal, traffic is something that still annoys us. It could even have a solution if the will was there to solve it. But we accept it.

While it's not what we like, we've grown accustomed to it. It's generally within the limits of our expectations. We allow extra time because we expect delays. Who's in charge of the traffic, after all? Who can make a difference? The government perhaps?

For most of us "the government" means a nonresponsive, nonspecific group of bureaucrats. No one is clearly accountable, and even if they were, how could we, average people, find our way through the labyrinth that is "the system" so that we could contact them.

This was part of the reason that I left the government (yes, I worked in a bureaucracy for a while). I wanted to be accountable. I wanted people to be able to talk directly to me about their challenges, and that wasn't necessarily how the average bureaucrat felt things should work. Me setting the precedent made them feel very vulnerable, and I became very unpopular (with the bureaucrats, of course).

We've all been lost in the paperwork and red tape of a bureaucracy at some time, totally unable to make our way through it to find someone we can talk to.

That's just one example of why many of us hesitate at using a capital G for Government: we don't feel they deserve it.

Back to being a Customer on a daily basis.

Will the traffic lead to the downfall of the government? Probably not. We've grown to expect and accept traffic delays as part of our daily lives. We're satisfied—until it reaches a level we don't expect. Even then, we can adapt to almost anything in time. Recent US Census data shows that the average commute for Californians increased by over 3 percent between 1990 and 2000. What on earth is it now? And when will Californians get sick of it?

We're still commuting, predominantly by car, and we're still getting stuck in ever-increasing traffic jams. But isn't that what you expect when you live in or near a city? So, I guess we're satisfied.

There we have it: Customer satisfaction. We experience it every day. Pretty much all that Customer satisfaction means is that the Customer Service we experience is no less than our expectations and often, due to continual exposure to poor Customer Service, our expectations are much less than we deserve. While we may not necessarily be happy about the level of service we are given, we don't see a viable alternative, and so we are satisfied.

This isn't a particularly good way to engender long-term Customer Loyalty, although it is an easy way to run a business

However, there's no guarantee that the Customers will come back to us next time. There is no sense of loyalty, no sense of ownership or partnership. They are merely "Customers" rather than "*Our* Customers." To them, we are just "a provider" rather than "*their* provider."

How then do we get our Customers to morally and emotionally partner with us? How do they become *our* Customer and we become *their* provider?

Could this require more than mere satisfaction on their part and some extra effort on our part? That can be an alien concept for some companies: putting in extra effort to gain extra rewards.

Let's explore this a little.

Let's look at one of the world's most romantic industries—travel. Okay, perhaps it's a little more romantic for some than others. While we discuss this, consider how these aspects of the passenger experience can be translated into your industry, your company, and your Customers' experiences.

Specifically let's look at air travel. By its very nature, air travel includes virtually every type of Customer Service:

- call centers;
- bookings and reservations (in person, over the phone, on the web, or through agents);
- inquiries and complaints;
- Customer Recovery;
- waiting areas, queuing, and boarding;
- dealing with delays and lost luggage;
- loyalty programs;
- pricing, packaging, and promoting;
- food and beverage service;
- comfort and hospitality;
- welcoming and saying good-bye;
- personal, terminal, and vehicle environments;
- timely delivery of people and goods;
- safety; and

- cleanliness and convenience.

This industry has the ability to get it either very very right or very very wrong.

In the next few examples, we'll explore how we can still be satisfied by low levels of Customer Service when every provider does the same thing. Then we'll see how it takes only a few simple changes by one company to cause people suddenly to realize that satisfaction isn't enough.

Airlines and airports are one of my favorite places to observe Customer interactions. You have to admire the design of airport departure lounges. (As an Australian, I often say things with my tongue planted firmly in my cheek. See if you can determine when.)

We, the people who are passengers on airliners and users of departure lounges, know that the number of seats in an average jet airliner is anywhere from 80 to more than 400, depending on the aircraft type. And a simple web search tells us that the Boeing 737, one of the most prevalent airliners in the world, carries between 100 and 180 passengers. A Boeing 747 carries more than 400. Why is it that airport authorities, and the architects they pay to design their facilities, persist in providing gate lounges with as few as 40 seats, or if you're really lucky, in an international terminal, maybe 100 seats.

Sure, we'll be sitting for a long time once we get on the plane; however, with the questionable punctuality of many airlines, I still like to be able to sit while I'm waiting to board an aircraft.

When I examined the theory behind departure lounge seating capacity, I found several academic papers that included a series of amazing formulae like these:

$$Q = A(t_b) = A(N/B)$$

followed by

$$A = \alpha[mS + m\ Q - S]$$

then

$$A \geq \alpha[mS + m\ N - S]$$

And, of course

$$\gamma_c = \alpha\gamma L(m_1 - m_2) + \gamma_s^{\,1}$$

This is absolutely amazing and a positively brilliant piece of work.

Now, the formulae above came from a very good paper entitled "Sizing the Airport Passenger Departure Lounge for the NLA" by Alexandre G. Barros and S. C. Wirasinghe from the University of Calgary's School of Civil Engineering. Having been a transportation planner in a previous life, I highly commend this paper. It is a great piece of engineering work with a comprehensive approach. I imagine that there are a number of similar papers that, in their own ways, address these design issues.

I present the above formulae not to help you design an airport or to critique any engineer's work, however to illustrate my point that a lot of effort and energy have gone into designing airport departure lounges, and yet many of us are still left standing.

No doubt, these and many other engineers and architects have spent a great deal of time and money trying to balance various competing interests, including money, space, time, and people. They do their best to optimize a situation and to satisfy everyone's needs.

---

1   The formulae are by no means comprehensive or completely within context and can be reviewed on http://www.schulich. ucalgary.ca/Civil/NLAircraft/TRBPaper.pdf, by anyone who is keenly interested in departure lounge design. Published in *Transportation Research Record* 1622 (1988): 13-21.

And there's that word again: *satisfy.*

In such instances, some additional common sense and a little extra money could go a long way toward improving the Customer Experience.

When it costs $300 million to $500 million dollars to construct an international airport and more than 30 million passengers use it each year, it would be nice to think that those passengers are important. If the airport is designed to last twenty years, that works out to less than one dollar per passenger use. Surely we can afford a few extra seats in the departure lounges if it means that our Customer will be more comfortable, more satisfied, and perhaps even happier.

> ### The Headsets.com Way—
> ### Maximizing Customer Convenience
>
> If Headsets.com were to design an airport, its approach could be as simple as finding out the largest aircraft likely to use that gate and have enough seats in the lounge for all of them. Oh, and of course, let's also make sure they're comfortable seats.
>
> Yes, it would be more expensive, however what price happiness? It may even mean that our Customers want to use our airport in preference to other airports.

An example of this is the level of staffing in the Headsets. com Customer Contact Center. They always provide more staff than necessary to answer the phones so a real person always answers within three rings. To ensure this, three electronic displays are positioned in the center for everyone to clearly see how many people are available and how many calls are in queue.

This display is also visible on everyone's computer desktop. Additionally, a captain (supervisor) works as a call optimizer to ensure that people are available to take Customers' calls, even if it means the facilities coordinator, the Customer Service Manager, the CFO, or even the CEO.

There's a no-questions-asked approach to this. Everyone watches the display and answers the calls when they're needed.

The Tides of Change

You might argue that I've ignored basic economics; however, I'd like you to consider what has been happening with some of the newer Asian and Middle Eastern air terminals in cities like Hong Kong, Singapore, and Dubai.

Museums, cinemas, even hotels have seats—plenty of seats. No longer are airports simply places where people wait to get on or off a flight; they have become venues providing a comprehensive visiting experience. Some of their personnel are even referred to as members of their Customer Experience Team.

These airports are now offering an alternative, and many international travelers are choosing to fly via them, rather than using the older, more traditional airports.

Even in these times of fiscal constraint, I know many executives who choose a longer flight with an airline that they like through a more passenger-focused airport that caters to their needs and desires, rather than shorter, less expensive trip.

A stunning example of this type of airport—one that has a symbiotic relationship with an airline of excellence—is Dubai International Airport and Emirates Airlines.

In the 1970s and early 1980s, the Dubai, Bahrain, and Abu Dhabi airports were the main Middle Eastern hubs. The endurance of the aircraft in those decades meant that flights between Europe and Asia/Australia generally needed to refuel at one of these airports. Likewise, flights between Africa and Asia would frequent these airports. Then, as longer-range aircraft developed, the importance of the Middle East as a refueling stop diminished significantly.

In 1983, Dubai International Airport handled some 3.5 million passenger movements. By 1986, this had only increased to 3.8 million passenger movements, an increase of less than 4 percent. The year 1986 saw the first decline in overall passenger movements, with a decrease of 1.5 percent recorded at Dubai.

Here's my personal experience with the Dubai of the 1980s:

Passengers would arrive very early, say at two or three in the morning, walk across a hot tarmac (yes, hot even at that time) escorted by armed guards into relatively small waiting areas with a couple of coffee carts and a magazine stand. If it hadn't been Arabian, I would have said Spartan!

I managed to catch up on my reading during these stopovers, although that was about all. We would sit there for two or three hours while our aircraft was refueled and catered, then happily re-board to continue our flight.

When we heard that new long-range aircraft permitted us to fly routes that stopped in Singapore and bypassed the Middle East, most of my colleagues and I rejoiced. Then, not a decade later, I arrived back in Dubai. This time my flight from London had only one stop: Dubai International Airport. Memories flooded back.

I arrived for my reading session armed with a tome substantial enough to negate any opportunity for additional cabin baggage. But I didn't have a chance to read it. (Based on a recent US experience, my next transit through LAX may afford me the opportunity.) Dubai International Airport is a Customer Service Experience that I commend to everyone. I was enthralled by the myriad of cafés, restaurants, retail outlets, and even a stand with duty-free luxury-car "guessing games."

Within its two-terminal complex (T3 has now been opened, and I'm sure that it will prove to be even more amazing), this award-winning airport (over seventy international awards to date) provides the traveler with

- fifty-four thousand square feet (about 5,400 square meters) of retail shopping;

- twenty-five food and beverage outlets from fast food to a la carte dining;
- a children's play area;
- a health club with swimming pool, Jacuzzi, and gym;
- a five-star hotel;
- two business centers;
- a medical center;
- and over fifteen lounges (business and airline) in addition to conference rooms accommodating up to sixty people—*plus* lots of comfortable seating.

Many business travelers, including me, now prefer to fly via Dubai rather than any other North American, European, or Middle Eastern airport. This is clearly illustrated by its increasing patronage, which is currently over 20 million passenger and 170,000 aircraft movements annually.

In the case of Dubai (the city, airport, and Emirates Airlines), the decision makers recognized a need to change, to adapt, and their solution was to provide their Customers (and the Customers of many other airports) with some much greater than satisfaction—and it most definitely has worked.

Dubai gives its Customers what they want and more. Everyone involved with the airport does their utmost to make life easy for their Customers. I'd never before had cleaning staff smile at me and say hello. In many countries, you feel privileged if you get a polite grunt.

Following close on Dubai's heels are Hong Kong International and Singapore Changi Airports. Each vies for the crown of perfection, continually pushing Customer Service to new heights—it's about money—our money. If travelers choose their airport (or your company) over others, there's money in it for the winner. Lots of money!

There are more of these new airport complexes on the way. I've mentioned Singapore and Hong Kong, and I understand that Seoul and Beijing are approaching the status of what ten years ago was unheard of.

In the United States, we generally continue to accept the inevitable: limited facilities, long lines, standing room only, airlines that are nickel and diming us, frequent delays, and possibly worst of all, grumpy staff. (Note: Dubai International was the first airport to uniformly enforce major financial penalties for airlines that did not depart on time.) We continue to fly, and very few of us ever complain.

Why?

It's a bit like the examples of traffic and the government that we previously discussed:

- What good would it do if we did complain?
- Who would we complain to? Who would listen to us—really listen to us?
- Would it make any difference?
- What else can we do? Flying is currently the most efficient method for traveling long distances quickly, and there are very few alternatives that we can choose from, particularly domestically.

The average passenger expects to be treated like this, and so is more or less satisfied. Whether you believe in "the power of attraction" or not, all of this can become a self-fulfilling prophesy.

Times can change though. Headsets.com changed from being a simple headset discounter to a world-class Customer Service Team, and in so doing moved the goal posts. And once a Customer has experienced true excellence, it's nearly impossible to get him or her to accept anything less.

Customer satisfaction is both relative and transitory. It is also comparative.

Just as our Customers can become numb to poor Customer Service, when they experience great Customer Service, they begin to remember the days of yore: the bygone days when Customers were important and were treated with respect and caring.

Once there is a benchmark to gauge service against, satisfaction can rapidly become dissatisfaction, and we, as business owners or operators, need to be on the winning side of that change. That is, we need to be the one setting the benchmark rather than being measured against it.

The catalyst for the swing from satisfaction to dissatisfaction can be big, small, or even the result of a cumulative effect. Sometimes it is simply that people have drawn the line because they have grown tired of the low level of Customer Service that they've been experiencing. However, more often it's because these people have been exposed to an alternative they prefer. Much of the current satisfaction with (or perhaps simply *acceptance of*) US air terminals and airlines is because most of them are pretty much the same, and a number of local users have never experienced better.

However, in the first half of 2008, news bulletins briefly flashed across our television screens that a recent survey[2] found that large numbers of US passengers had chosen not to fly, costing US airlines several billion dollars in lost income. The reasons not to fly were said to include

- increased prices for lower levels of service;
- flight delays and cancellations;
- low levels of Customer Service; and
- the nickel-and-diming of Customers—for example, being charged for any luggage other than carry-on and paying for meals (even if they're just cardboard boxes of chips and cookies on a five-hour flight).One airline in Europe has even threatened to charge a fee for the use of aircraft lavatories!

The alternatives that these Customers have been choosing in preference to flying include

- telephone and videoconferencing;
- train or car travel for shorter-distance trips;
- local rather than distant vacations; and
- simply not traveling.

On the brighter side, the recent groundswell against the nickel-and-diming resulted in the following comedy skit in which the cabin crew asked:

---

2 I've been unable to source this survey; however, its reported findings do not surprise me.

Would you like a drink? That'll be $5.

Would you like some ice with that? That'll be $2.

Would you like a glass? ...

The Headsets.com Way

If Headsets.com were running one of the above airlines, rather than charge someone extra for luggage, they'd probably promote an offer to provide discounted fares to people who choose to travel only with carry-ons.

So, what does all of this have to do with giving your Customers a capital C?

A lot. It means that the American public (and generally Customers around the world) are beginning to stand up for themselves and demand improvements in the way they are treated. Admittedly some Customers are more advanced in their demands than others, and this trend is more obvious in some industries than others.

While some people are prepared to pay more for better service, others, who are more sensitive to the vagaries of the economic climate, are becoming more selective in who they spend their money with, and they demand both competitive pricing and better service.

Likewise, many companies are tightening their financial belts and often feel that this means cutting corners to cut costs. Something that many companies seem to miss is that Customer Service Excellence doesn't need enormous capital outlay, however merely a capital letter—a capital C.

Many of the principles behind making your Customers a priority can be implemented at minimal cost. All that is required is a repositioning of the company's mindspace (or culture, if you like), a review of standard documents, more selective recruitment, improved training, and maybe rewards for people who offer their Customers great service.

There needn't be a lot of money involved to achieve excellence in Customer Service. Success with your new approach requires careful planning, determination, and a lot of energy and patience.

Remember that it's often the little things that can make a big difference to the Customer Experience. And, of course, death (or the devil, if you prefer) really is in the details.

With air travel, a small group of airlines has recognized that people want more than their expectations met; they want them exceeded. They want to be pleasantly surprised every time they fly with that airline. Virgin, Emirates, and Singapore Airlines have recognized that Customers want and deserve more. They also know that Customer Service Excellence can be a key to differentiating them from other airlines.

This is exactly the niche that Headsets.com happily occupies with its approach to Customer Service. Headsets.com places its Customers above everything else.

It is within the power of each and every one of us to provide Customer Service Excellence—genuine Customer Love—to everyone that we deal with every time we deal with him or her. And the people we help, wittingly or unwittingly, pass on some of their enjoyment to the next person that they deal with, and so on and so on. The multiplication effect can be incredible.

Not only do we have the ability, we also have the responsibility, to do this.

The world is a drab and depressing enough place, often seemingly filled with injustice, sadness, wars, and crime. So why not help change things, even just a little, by the way we treat the people around us—our Customers.

Something that Headsets.com does well is recognize the numerous categories of Customers—some obvious, some not. A key to understanding Headsets.com's holistic approach to Customer Service is to consider it within the context of the larger realm of Customers—what I refer to as the "in-Customers." This realm consists of five categories of Customer, which include everyone that you will ever deal with. With this in mind, Customer Service Excellence—true Customer Love—becomes a powerful business tool whose principles can be applied to any business situation.

The Five Customer Categories

Here are the categories of in-Customers that I refer to:

- **In-coming Customers**—often referred to as external Customers, these are the ones we are the most familiar with and the most concerned about. They buy from us by walking into our store or office, calling us, or writing to us because they want our product or service.

Most Customer Service books are geared toward serving these Customers because they are the ones who directly give us money.

However, if we focus solely on them, we miss out on numerous opportunities to improve our bottom line. For example, treating our team better will result in higher levels of performance, and working with, rather than against, our suppliers will mean better deals and more reliable deliveries. These are some of the other aspects of Customer Service that are often neglected and yet are an essential component of a genuinely comprehensive Customer Experience Package.

So, *always* remember to love *all* your Customers in *all ways*.

- **In-ternal Customers**—while these are fairly obvious, they sometimes slip under our radar. They are the people who are in our team, both those that deal directly with our in-coming Customers and those that help to keep the wheels turning internally. If we've put the energy and effort into hiring Mr. and Ms. Rights, let's also do our best to keep them motivated and happy. What a waste it would be to lose even one of them before they've had the opportunity to contribute to our growth, development, and profitability, let alone after we've trained them to contribute fully.

- **In-verse Customers**—these are the people and companies that we are Customers to. Most people call them suppliers. Why do I suggest that we apply the principles of Customer Love to them that we pay money to? Simple. If we treat them well, they're a lot more likely to treat us well. And don't you just love it when you're a priority Customer too?

- **In-terpersonal Customers**—this is really starting to take Customer Love to a whole new level. I suggest that we should try to make a difference in our own lives and in the world as a whole by applying these same incredible principles of service to our Family and Friends (note the capitalization). All of the principles of making every one of our Customers a Customer with a capital C translate easily into our personal lives. When we apply them, almost magically, our lives become easier, less stressful, and more fun. That means that we'll feel better and the people around us will feel better, and our workplace will benefit from it, almost as if it's by osmosis.

- Finally there's the **In-you Customer**—*you!* This one is *really* important! With the world's ever-increasing levels of stress and stress-related illness, don't you want to give yourself a little Customer Love as well?

When you feel good about yourself, you help your Customers feel good, they enjoy working with you, and you enjoy working with them ... and on it goes. *Have fun!*

Each Customer category has a direct impact on our performance and the long-term health and profitability of our company. Courting Customers with Customer Love will help us achieve higher levels of excellence for our in-coming Customers, which, in turn, will to the following:

- make them happier;
- encourage their loyalty;

- help them buy more from us;

- encourage them to spread the word to other potential Customers; and

- make us happier because our bottom line will continue to increase.

The effect is like compound interest and, as Albert Einstein said, "The most powerful force in the Universe is compound interest". Wouldn't you like your company to experience that type of power in the marketplace?

With luck, more and more companies will embrace the concept of treating every stakeholder (its service team, credit control, management, suppliers, investors, as well as the buying public) as it's very, very special Customers. I don't mind what their reason is, even if it's only because the return on investment (RoI) is unbelievably high, as long as we're all treated as very special human beings. Let's face it; there's not much monetary investment involved in replacing a c with a C. The challenge is ensuring that the associated mindset is achieved from the very start.

Hopefully one day we (as Customers) will not need to be dragged kicking and screaming to the phone to deal with the power supplier, cable provider, or credit card company. Rather we will relish the experience and look forward to how great it feels when we are uniformly treated as a Customer with a capital C. Or even, perhaps a capital P— People.

What Will I Do to Help My Team Recognize the Five Customer Categories?

---

a) Now—yes right away!

....

....

....

....

....

b) By the end of this week

....

....

....

....

....

c) By the end of this month

....

....

....

....

....

CHAPTER 4

Questions with a Capital Q

As with the Headsets.com experience, once you've decided that your goal is to provide your Customers with the most astounding Customer Service they can imagine, you need to know what they can imagine.

The question is, how?

By asking questions—clear, simple questions to all of your Customer categories.

Ask questions like these for you and your team:

- What do you want to sell?
- Why do you want to sell it?
- Who would want to buy it? (You can and should also ask your potential Customers this question.)

And ask these for your potential and/or existing Customers:

- Would they like to buy it?
- How would they like to buy it?
- What would help them want to buy it from you?
- How much would they pay for it?
- What would they like to buy with it?

- What could you do to help them buy it?

- What would they be prepared to pay extra for? And, of course, what wouldn't they?

In other words, the traditional who, what, when, where, why, and how that we continually encounter in our daily lives.

Or, if you're a fan of TV crime shows, you could make it as simple as means, motive, and opportunity:

- Who has the means—both economic and physical— to buy your products?

- What is their motivation for buying it?

- How can you give them the opportunity to buy it from you?

As Mike Faith says, "It isn't rocket science!"

The original 1997 concept for Mike's headset sales company was simply to sell telephone headsets quickly, easily, and cheaply. It was pretty much a discounter simply selling telephone headsets at as low a price as could be sustained. It was a fairly conventional web- and telephone-based operation that, more or less, satisfied its Customers.

Sales went reasonably well, and the company grew at a reasonable rate. It was all pretty reasonable. However, I've never known Mike to remain reasonable for long. He, as always, clearly wanted more for his company. It had to be something special. Unreasonable—perhaps. Visionary— definitely. So he started asking more questions.

The next question to be asked was, what do more and special mean?

And then what were their Customers' wants, needs, and desires.

That was the start of being special. Soon began the cultural shift that eventually led the company into a completely different realm, an area in which it was to have no rivals, no competition, not even peers. Why? Because, simply put, no one would do what Headsets.com did as well as they did it.

They were to discover Customer Love; they were about to venture into the mindspace that capitalizes *Customer(s)* in more ways than one.

None of this would have happened if they hadn't asked those questions and continued asking them to this very day. They'd already asked themselves what they wanted to sell—telephone headsets—and why they wanted to sell them—to share the benefits of headsets and make to profit at the same time.

The next two questions that had to be asked were these: Who would want to buy them? And how would they like to buy them?

So, they asked.

They asked people who had headsets. They asked people who didn't have headsets. They asked people they knew, and they asked people they didn't know. They asked people who worked with Headsets.com. They asked people who didn't work with Headsets.com.

Basically they asked anyone that they could gain cheap, easy, reliable access to.

My advice to you?

Do the same thing—go out and ask people. Find out who is buying your types of products. Find out why they're buying them and why they aren't. Find out what would get these people to buy them. Importantly, find out what would entice them to buy these products from you.

Take this to the next level by finding out what they need, want, and desire. Then find ways to delivery this to them unfailingly and to make it an even better Customer Experience every time.

The Headsets.com Way

How did Headsets.com do it?

There's no magic formula, just a lot of work.

They have four basic approaches to finding out what their existing and potential Customers want:

1) **Customer roundtables**—Customers sit around a table, eat a nice dinner, and talk about what they expect from companies that sell headsets. (Although I have said that Headsets.com has no competition, they are aware that there are some companies out there that do try to sell telephone headsets.) Originally Headsets.com did these roundtables in general terms; now their focus is on what their Customers would like in terms of service; how their team could make it better; and new products that might be of interest to their Customers.

It's incredible what you can learn over a simple dinner and a chat. I think that a key to the Headsets.com approach is that they keep it informal. It's more like a quiet dinner with friends, where the conversation just happens to turn to Headsets and Customer Service, than an interview panel. They invite all types of people—their frequent Customers, their less frequent Customers, and people who have never bought anything from them.

Always remember the value of speaking with people who have bought products like yours from someone else.

Another critical element in their approach to roundtables is to remain completely open-minded, to value everyone's opinions, and then to see how they can be incorporated into the Headsets.com culture and their approach to Customer Service. As Mike puts it, "Your Customer may not always be right; however, they are never wrong."

2. **Customer surveys**—Headsets.com sends out Customer surveys with every item purchased and rewards all Customers who return a survey with a discount on their next purchase. (These are the surveys that provided the basis for the all-important Customer Service Excellence Ratings that I mentioned earlier.)

The surveys ask Customers about

- their overall experience;

- the individual team member they spoke with;

- the company website;

- the product support team (if the Customer used product support);

- whether they'd like to be contacted personally by a member of the Headsets.com team;

- whether they'd recommend Headsets.com to a friend;

- if there is anything that they'd like the company to change;

- any general comments on the company and their Customer Service Experience; and

- how their team could improve the Customer Experience.

While this sounds like a lot of information, it's laid out very simply, and for the most part it's quick and easy because of multiple-choice answers.

However, you can always encourage your participants to add to the feedback in their own words; there are often real gems hidden among the various tidbits of information.

3. **Ask the team**—everyone at Headsets.com is continually encouraged to contribute ideas. They can just walk up to a manager and tell him or her, make a suggestion in their weekly meeting, or contact Mike personally. They also have an electronic suggestion box from which the best suggestions are rewarded and the ideas published in the weekly e-newsletter.

   One of the most gratifying things I find in my work with Headsets.com is that I can make a suggestion on Tuesday morning and see it being used on Tuesday afternoon.

4. **Ask questions—lots of questions**—we've devoted a large component of this chapter to asking questions and for good reason: in addition to the roundtables and team suggestions, the people at Headsets.com continually ask people what they want. Friends, family, people at business functions, conferences, parties, even unsuspecting passengers sitting next to them on a plane or a train—no one is exempt! It's not at all uncommon to see Mike, in particular, at a social event or business function, talking to people about Customer Service and telephone headsets. I've even known him and his team to arrive at functions armed with a variety of different headsets for people to

try. (They really do love their headsets and what Headsets. com is about).

As a tribute to this, the walls of the Headsets.com offices are dotted with photographs of unsuspecting people that Mike has convinced to try on a headset—some famous, some slightly more obscure—and they are all invited to give him feedback.

In terms of the use of surveys, there are definitely quite a few things to remember. The formulation of surveys is a very specific science, and possibly even an art. It is possible to create surveys that give you exactly the information you don't want. You can manipulate the wording, phrasing, and positioning of questions in such a way that you obtain information that is absolutely useless to you unless you simply want to validate that everything you are doing is "just fine and dandy." However, if you really want to use the results to help you improve, always take care to study the subject extensively or employ an expert to design your surveys.

Even after you have developed your perfect survey, be prepared to help it evolve. As the responses come in, examine what they are saying both in terms of how they can help you and how the questions might be redesigned to provide you with more valuable information. Clearly the response rate is important. So, always explore and re-explore ways to improve your response rate. Consider the following:

- Include online submission as an option. This is an increasingly electronic world and can significantly increase your response rate.

- Keep the questions clear and concise. Avoid ambiguity at all costs, and make it obvious that the survey will be quick and easy to complete.

- Make it easy for your Customers to answer, and whenever possible, provide your Customers with the opportunity to add their own comments.

- Ideally keep your survey to one page (or screen for e-surveys) so your Customers can clearly see that it will involve only a little of their time. I recognize that this will not always be practical, as some surveys require a lot more information. If this is the case, clearly specify the time that the survey will take, each Customer's progress through the survey, and that there is a worthwhile reward for them at the end. And always thank your Customer for their help.

That brings us to rewards or incentives.

- To improve your survey response rate, provide a tangible incentive for your Customers. Some companies include the pen that the survey is completed with or a voucher, while others offer a series of prize draws. The general rule of thumb is that the less valuable, less accessible, and less tangible the incentive, the less chance you have of obtaining a significant response rate of valuable, reliable information. In the case of Headsets.com, the incentive is a discount voucher toward the Customer's next purchase.

- Incentives aren't as expensive as many people think. Naturally, the higher the value of the discount voucher, the greater the redemption rate is likely to be. Think about it for a moment: when was the last time that you used that dollar off your next purchase of X Farm Brand turkey?

Many people will be too embarrassed to redeem a small voucher unless prompted by the person serving them. (Note here that Headsets.com's Core Customer Service Team members are trained to prompt their Customers to use their vouchers. That's really going an extra mile for your Customers!)

Naturally, in tougher economic times, the redemption rate will increase, however it is highly unlikely to reach unmanageable levels—unless you make it an offer too good to refuse, such as a free car with every fifty dollars' worth of groceries purchased. If you're going to journey down that road, perhaps you need a *very* different kind of help than what's provided in this book.

Clearly Headsets.com asks a lot of questions.

One question that I've found some other companies a little hesitant to ask is, "How did you feel about your overall experience?" or "How did you feel about the company representative that you dealt with?"

When I mentioned this questions to some companies, their excuses for not asking it included the following:

- It's a bit like a written reference that is given to an employee when they leave—who's going to write anything nasty?

- It's like an "other comments" question; no one pays attention to them.

- A couple of comments like that won't affect the way we operate, so why bother?

Well, if that's your company's mindset, then you're absolutely right. They won't make a difference, and you are unlikely to grow, evolve, and continue to excel in your Customers' eyes

However, for if you are interested in changes that will lead to improved Customer Loyalty and an improved bottom line, let's consider the value of answers to these types of questions: "How did you feel about your overall experience?" or "How did you feel about the company representative that you dealt with?" You'll note I've used the word *feel* rather than *think*. In my opinion, the greatest value of a Customer Experience is the emotive responses it evokes in your Customer.

Emotions are a key factor in the Customer Experience. It's about how they *feel* when each of their transactions has concluded—how they feel when they put down the phone, leave the store, drive from the gas station, or get off the plane.

The answers to these types of questions can, of course, be used anyway you choose. However, these are their main value:

- Providing your Customers with an increased sense of ownership in your Customer Service process. The way to engender this sense of ownership is by contacting all Customers who make suggestions that you act on, telling them what you are going to do to act on their suggestion (or concern), thanking them for their contribution to improving your company, and maybe even rewarding them for their effort.

- Helping your management team identify and act on trends early, be they individual or company-wide.

- Providing you with the opportunity to give well-deserved praise to specific individuals or your team as a whole.

- Perhaps even providing you with an opportunity to give recognition to your great Customers. Remember that you can also ask your team for their take on the Customer Experience.

The Headsets.com Way

Every Thursday afternoon, the Headsets.com family gets together for a meeting. They are updated on new products and processes and sometimes given additional or refresher training. They *always* read Customer Feedback that was received the previous week.

These are typical Headsets.com's Customer comments:

Customer representative was a port in a storm, water in a desert, and a great Headset Specialist. A perfect 10!

Nancy B
Greenbrae, California

Without a doubt, the best company I have ever worked with. You have me as a lifetime Customer.

Kristine J
Tucker, Georgia

At Headsets.com, you guys are truly the best. I have had nothing however wonderful experiences in dealing with you: whether it was an original purchase, a warranty issue, or a product support issue. You are a rare breed, and you should be proud of it.

Amir M
Salt Lake City, Utah

The morale building and validation that goes along with everyone hearing these comments and sharing their own recent experiences with their Customers has to be seen to be believed. When, for three to five minutes, they share these comments and applaud the truly great ones, the energy and enthusiasm in the room puts most companies and their very best Christmas Bonus Giving Day to shame, let alone their regular staff meetings.

What Will I Do to Improve My Understanding of My Customers' Wants, Needs, and Desires?

a) Now—yes right away!

....

....

....

....

....

b) By the end of this week

....

....

....

....

....

c) By the end of this month

....

....

....

....

....

CHAPTER 5

Hiring with a Capital H

A key factor in the success of Headsets.com is their firm belief that they need to hire the best people in order to achieve the best Customer Experience. Training the best to be even better so that they can become the very best.

Many companies—I'd suggest perhaps as many as 90 percent, consider Customer Service to be an entry-level position. That's why as a nation we currently experience some of the lowest service standards we've ever had. One of the things that makes Headsets.com different in the retail industry is that they consider Customer Service to be their frontline—equally as important as management, technical support, and consultants. It is their primary interface between Customers, company, and products. It's where all the important factors meet—or don't meet if things go wrong.

In many ways, it's the most important function in a company, and truly great Customer Service people are hard to find.

The Headsets.com Way—Hiring

Headsets.com's reputation precedes them. Applicants already know that this company is serious about great Customer Service before they apply for a position, and if an applicant doesn't, it becomes apparent during the initial stages of the recruitment process.

The advertisement itself is daunting. First, it makes it very clear that you have to be special; only about one applicant out of every one hundred is selected.

It explains that they are looking for a very special kind of person with the following characteristics:

- An ability to create an emotional connection with a Customer on the telephone is crucial.

- Excellent communication and listening skills are essential.

- An ability to accommodate rather than dominate must be an intrinsic part of his or her personality.

A successful applicant must also have the following characteristics:

- a high amount of patience;

- a strong attention to detail;

- the desire to work very hard in a friendly team;

- the ability and longing to learn and to give unparalleled Customer Service;

- a great telephone manner;

- an extremely reliable and consistent personality;

- an enjoyment of an early start time;

- a willingness to deal with phones ringing constantly all day; and

- an eagerness to develop new skills.

Breaking the mold of traditional application processes, the company asks applicants to send an email with the subject line "Customer Service is Awesome!" and a brief description of a positive experience that they've had with another company when they were a Customer.

Headsets.com wants to make its own judgment on suitability and so insists that applicants not include résumés, references, or any other attachments; those who do automatically cull themselves from the interview process.

If that isn't enough, there is a four-stage interview process spanning about two weeks, including several telephone and in-person interviews. These telephone interviews include chats with various managers, the CEO, and the company's recruitment manager. During the process, applicants are asked questions like the length of a well-know type of car and which state Massachusetts is in?[1]

And, yes, there's more. There's even a telephone interview with yours truly, the company voice coach, who could be anywhere in the world, so you have to work out time zones, etc.

To raise the stakes a little more and to throw them a curve ball, I ask prospective new hires to make strange sounds and to repeat tongue twisters so that I can hear their telephone voice and see how adaptable they are and what their attention to detail is like—through a sort of actor's audition process.

Finally, those who make it through the telephone and personal interviews spend a full day in the Customer Contact Center with people who are really doing the job.

Ultimately, a prospective new hire to Headsets.com speaks with upward of fifteen people in the company, and each and every one of them is asked for their opinion, even if they only spoke with that person in the lunchroom. Everyone's opinion is valued, because it's the people who work there that know the culture and the type of person that is, or isn't, a great fit.

It's a matter of recognizing how important your frontline is and what the consequences are if you place the wrong person in the wrong position.

Consider it this way: if your Customer Service people are brilliant and they serve their Customers to an amazingly high level, treating them as though they deserve a capital C, then not only will you have a lot of happy return Customers, you'll also have fewer complaints and concerns from your Customers. That means less resources you need to devote to

---

3   Yes, I know Massachusetts is a state, and it's interesting to hear which candidates forget that when they're under pressure.

dealing with something that none of us relishes, particularly managers and supervisors.

Ultimately, hiring the right people for the right job means that everyone will be happier—internally and externally.

You can hire the very best people in the world, however if you don't provide them with the best possible training, you might just as readily have spent fifty dollars on a local newspaper or web advertisement and accepted the first ten people who applied. Or perhaps you could have bypassed people altogether and simply installed a cost-effective voice recognition software package. Without the training, how will your team ever know to give your Customers a capital C, let alone what it means?

At Headsets.com, the initial training process is an intensive two weeks of solid culture, process, and products. While all new hires are given complete support from everyone involved, they really have to have their heart in it. Considering the efficiency of the interview process and intensity of this training period (which includes a full day with the CEO), you pretty much know by day 10 whether you've chosen Mr. or Ms. Right. In fact, Our New Hires (the company recognizes the importance of its new recruits by using this name for them) know it too.

While the hiring process is intensive and extensive, it is not infallible. I've never come across one that is. The less than 5 percent of new hires that don't make the grade generally know it themselves by the start of the second week.

The Headsets.com Way—Training

The two-week training program is organic and has been evolving for the past seven years or so, being slightly modified after each group of new hires.

Training commences with some introductory information about the company: its background, mission, objectives, beliefs, and culture. This is when the concept of giving every one of your Customers a capital C is introduced—day 1. From that point onward, every Headsets.com document that they write, read, or refer to uses a capital C for Customer. Any other especially important person is treated likewise (for example, Our New Hires, Our Core Customer Service Team, Our Shipping Team).

On day 1, in addition to meeting their training manager (who runs their day-to-day training), they're introduced to key members of the Headsets.com team and their own personal trainers/mentors.

From then on, the training program is split into units of theory and practical application:

- Product knowledge—by the time the tenth day of training has concluded, each of our new hires has personally used each of the major models of headset sold by the company (and many of the more obscure ones as well).

- Computer processes—including placing orders, tracking orders, and setting up accounts for their Customers.

- Language and communication culture—including a series of role-playing calls where I take them through various scenarios and Customer Types, regardless of where I am in the world at the time.

- Daily practical live call time—spent with experienced members of our Customer Service Team, in which each new hire's responsibility gradually increases—from listening in to using the database while an experienced team member does the talking, to talking with the Customer while the team member enters information on their computer. Next comes paired training with two of our new hires working as a team, then ultimately solo time under supervision. (From my side, it's fantastic to see a process like this working and to watch their confidence increase exponentially daily.)

- "The Day with Mike Faith"—Mike personally spends an entire day with the new team. During this day, he gives them his own personal insights and continually quizzes them.

Finally, after ten days of intensive training, unless everyone that has worked with a new hire is totally satisfied with his or her progress, he or she doesn't "graduate." This person may go onto the phone under supervision and be asked to repeat or add to some of the training; however, he or she will not have graduated to being a full-fledged Customer Care Expert.

Okay, so you've hired the right people, you've developed your training program, and you've trained them—now what?

Make sure that it has worked!

How do you know that you've got it right? Simple—your Customers will tell you.

Every week, hundreds of Customer surveys are returned to Headsets.com with the most amazing comments. They go from personal accolades like:

> "Chris was such a laugh, and he sold me the best headsets that I could imagine."

Or

> "Josh just blew me away with his product knowledge. Everything I asked he knew, and even some things that I didn't know to ask."

And

> "I wish every company had Headsets. com's service platform."

Or, even something as simple and elegant as

> "You guys ROCK!!!!"

These comments tell me that Headsets.com has got it right. Their Customers and their team are all Mr. or Ms. Right— after all, in my totally unbiased opinion, they all rock!

Comments from your Customers can tell you what you need to know. These can be through formal feedback on survey forms or in focus groups, comments that you pick up as you listen to sample recorded calls (you do record a sample of your calls, don't you?) or informal comments by Customers that you occasionally meet socially or otherwise.

To give you a feel for the type of responses that Headsets. com receives, below are a few more examples from the literally hundreds of comments received each week. Believe it, or not, I've grabbed this selection from the over twenty pages of Customer Comments that are included on the Headsets.com website.

Thank you for caring about all of your Customers. Some companies don't care as much about their smaller clients; however Headsets.com doesn't alter its service at all, regardless of the total amount spent.

Chantel A
Houston, Texas

Since I was unsure which headsets would work with our phones, the live chat option was fantastically helpful!

Cynthia S
Winston Salem, North Carolina

Like many executives, I tend to do much of my pre-purchase product research online and then prefer to buy the product in a retail store where I can get it the same day or hold it in my hands. Today I used your wonderful comparison engine to narrow down which headset would best fit my needs, printed out a couple of model numbers, and jumped in my car to the local retail outlets. After spending ninety minutes of my valuable time driving around in the hot sun to four different stores, speaking by cell phone with retail call center operators in India who had no idea if the store I was driving to had the product in stock or not, I gave up. On the way back to the office, I did what I should have done in the first place. I placed a two-minute call to 1-800-HEADSETS (800) 432-3738. The call was answered quickly by a person on-location who confirmed the model would work for me and that it would be at my office the next day. If you're looking for a headset for yourself or for your entire office staff, you're not going to save any additional money by buying locally. In fact, you will pay more because your time is money. I was very pleased with my buying experience and can highly recommend Headsets.com to anyone who needs to buy.

Adam B
Beaverton, Oregon

I called one day and the next day my headsets arrived—how do you improve on that?

Gene B
Redmond, Washington

If your headset service continues to be as excellent as our first contact, you'll be seeing many more headset orders!

Tami B
Tigard, Arizona

Your Headset specialists are awesome, and I mean awesome. Upper most professionalism. I give you a 100 percent!

Debra W
Raleigh, North Carolina

The Customer Service your company offers is exceptional. Always courteous, knowledgeable, and helpful with their headset recommendations.

Jean M
Cheshire, Connecticut

The Customer rep was fantastic, pleasant, helpful, and efficient. Other headset companies could learn from Headsets.com!

Rick S.
New Enterprise, Pennsylvania

I could easily say Best Customer Service consistently since 1998. I will always do business with your headset company.

Yvonne O
Honolulu, Hawaii

What Will I Do to Ensure That I Hire, Train, and Retain the Best People?

a) Now—right away!

....

....

....

....

....

b) By the end of this week

....

....

....

....

....

c) By the end of this month

....

....

....

....

....

CHAPTER 6

Company Culture
with a Capital Y *(for Yes)*

A large component of Headsets.com's training focuses on company culture. As you've made it this far in the book, you must already be aware that a pivotal feature of the Headsets.com culture is what they call Customer Love, including giving their Customers a capital C.

These are the key considerations when building a Customer-centric company:

- You have the right people in place, and they have the same goals. These goals must be Customer-focused because they genuinely believe this is where their personal future lies.

- Every member of your team must have a genuine desire to achieve Customer Service Excellence, and it must be applied uniformly across the board.

- If the people that you have onboard aren't "true believers," you're going to have to make a choice: either put in the effort and energy to help these people evolve, or help them evolve out of the company. To some extent, the choice will be yours; to some extent, it will be theirs.

- If cultural change is required, it starts at the top. If your frontline team sees your managers walking the walk rather than just talking the talk, they'll buy in much more readily.

- If you're an existing company, remember that change takes time.

- Cultures are subject to evolution. Establish what you think your culture should be then be prepared to help it grow and evolve as you find out more about what your Customers want.

- Keep trying to find out more! Then apply the new information. It's impossible to continually exceed your Customers' expectations if you don't know how those expectations evolved.

- Be open to new ideas.

Discovering What Your Customers Want

It's a bit like romance. That's probably why Headsets.com often refers to Customer Love when they're discussing how they treat their Customers.

Customers come in all shapes, sizes, and styles, and to excel in true Customer Love you need to court your Customers, each and every one of them, in their own unique ways.

In my younger "going a courtin' days," I would first find out what the particular girl of my dreams wanted. I figured that it was pretty pointless taking my poetry reading and cinnamon-stick-dipping hot chocolate drinker Jennifer to a football match. Likewise, when Carlie came along with her love of the outdoors and a taste for happy hour beer and meatballs, it didn't even briefly cross my mind to take her to the book club reading of John Donne's poetry. Well, to be truthful, it did, because of the impish side of me wanted to see how the librarians would react.

Then there were Julie and Sally and Mary and ... you get the picture. Each one was very different; however there was one common factor: you don't get far in courtship if you don't know what the other party wants.

This applies to both all our Customers—In-coming, In-ternal, In-verse, and In-you, just as well as it does to our In-terpersonal Customers

Clearly, in finding Mr. or Ms. Right (the members of our Customer Service Team) we've established the basics and know that we have the right people in place. Still, courtship is the time to explore their needs further and ensure that we really know what they want. Then we build the trust that we are going to deliver it—every time.

The reality is that your Customers are a bit more predictable than my Jennifer, Carlie, Sally, or even Natasha. (I just threw Natasha in to see if you were paying attention.) We can be pretty sure that no matter what we sell, Customers will, at the very least, want

- to be treated with respect;
- to deal with a friendly human being;
- to buy a product at a reasonable price, although they may be prepared to pay more for extra benefits;
- to experience positive, friendly, and professional behavior; and
- to enjoy the experience.

Then it's up to you to determine what specifics apply to your Customers, and each member of your Customer Service Team can take it even further by identifying the unique needs of their individual Customers (both their material and their psychological needs).

The Headsets.com Way?—Knowing What Your Customers Want

It's pretty simple. After asking a lot of questions and applying some common sense, Headsets.com decided that, all in all,

Customers want to be treated the way that you want to be treated when you're a Customer.

It may not be rocket science, however get it wrong and it can definitely blow up in your face.

Okay, that done, how do you build this into your company culture?

Clearly each company should develop its own approach to implementing cultural change, which will depend on many factors:

- the type of company and its products and services;
- the existing company culture;
- the Customer base;
- how Customers access the company;
- the types of people in it, including the ratio of old guard to new talent, staff turnover, and how readily the existing team can adopt new approaches (you

can teach old dogs new tricks, however it helps if
you can scatter a few new dogs among them); and

- the creativity of management in finding fresh
  approaches to implementing, fostering, and
  encouraging change.

Regardless of how these factors pan out in your company,
one factor remains constant: it will take time, energy, and
emotional investment to effect genuine change.

The Headsets.com Way? —Cultural Uptake

At Headsets.com, everyone is immersed in their culture
from the moment they enter the office or begin to talk
with someone. There are innumerable banners and posters
proclaiming the importance of their brand of Customer Love;
training manuals, posters, and panels proclaim it throughout
their offices. As you walk through the front door, your eyes
are drawn to "At Headsets.com we Love our Customers."

This phrase is the very center of their organization, and it
has helped them to grow at a rate of around 25 percent for
six years.

Then there's the language. Everyone you speak with (whether
you're a Customer on the phone, a trainer, a consultant, a
prospective new hire) uses unwaveringly positive, friendly,
helpful language. As well as this, you'll never hear anyone
complain about a Customer.

From the first moment of the morning to the last moment of
the afternoon, everyone lives the culture.

"We Love Our Customers"

> *"Customers Come First"*
>
> *"Give 'em the Pickle"(meaning to go that extra mile for your Customers – I take no credit for this it was justifiably made famous by Customer Service Guru Bob Farrell long before I came along)*
>
> When everyone around you is passionate and completely immersed in this type of energetic, contagious approach to life, you can't help however to absorb it, as if by osmosis.
>
> Next thing you know, you've bought into the Headsets. com company culture and you're spelling Customer with a capital C.

Your company culture has been established. Your team has enthusiastically bought in. Now you need to keep it fresh, evolving and responding to the changing needs and desires of your Customers and the world at large.

How?

Try the five Ms: Mention, Measure, Monitor, Motivate, and Manage. (These are very much Mike's brainchild, I've only helped adapt them).

Once you know exactly what your Customers want, you can't achieve anything if you keep it to yourself.

- **Mention It**—to your team and to your Customers. Tell everyone that this is what their Customers want and this is what you are going to deliver to them— and then some! Then tell your Customers that you understand that this is what they want and this is how you're going to give it to them. Then tell them that you'd love them to tell you how it's going and if there's anything else they'd like you to do for them.

- **Measure It**—Find ways to quantify how well your team delivers Customer Love (establish metrics). To engender a sense of ownership, responsibility and accountability, involve your team in establishing the metrics.

- **Monitor It**—Keep track of how well your company, your operational teams, and the individuals in those teams are doing by monitoring the metrics that you've established.

- **Motivate to Improve It**—Provide rewards for consistently meeting—or better yet, exceeding—the metrics that you've established. Provide these to individuals, teams, and even the whole company, if it warrants it. Match the rewards to the effort and outcome.

- **Manage It**—Continue the search for new ways to help your Customers: ask more questions and seek new ideas from both your Customers and your team. See if you can find new, better, more exciting ways to leave your Customers wondering how much more you can possibly do for them.

The Headsets.com Way? —The Five Ms

Once Headsets.com had established what it's Customers wanted and what the company needed to achieve, they developed a set of performance metrics.

They gauged their success as a company and the success of their individual Customer Service Team members by including a survey form with every item sold. This led to their now ubiquitous Customer Service Excellence Rating.

As the company grew to understand their Customers' desires better, these metrics evolved to encompass a broader range of criteria, which now include the following:

- Customer Service Excellence Rating: based on Customer surveys set at a minimum target of ten excellents to one non-excellent.
- Answer rate of telephone calls: every call must be answered by a real person within three rings.
- Response times for emails and live-person chats.
- Attendance and punctuality: like most companies, they'd like everyone to be at work on time every time.
- Call conversion: the number of calls that result in either a new account being set up or the sale of a product. (Without Customers buying their products, how long would Headsets.com stay viable and how would they have Customer Service benchmarks to gauge the rest of the world by?)
- Shipping accuracy: there isn't much point to being brilliant on the phone or the online chat if Customers don't get the right product on the day they've been promised.
- And, naturally, the dollar value of sales: the company is, after all, in the business of making money.

The Customer Service Excellence Rating

This rating is based on responses to Customer Service Surveys and is used as a tool to find out what Customers want and how successfully the Customer Service Teams are at delivering this.

How is this different from other companies?

While many companies send out surveys to their Customers that ask if their experience was poor, fair, good, very good, or excellent, most companies are satisfied with anything better than fair. Some are fine with fair because their goal is for their Customers not to have a *bad* experience.

This may seem like semantics, however there is a mindset associated with this type of statement that will continually inhibit excellence in such a company. I cannot expound too vigorously the importance of language in achieving a culture of excellence (and success).

Often the reason that the line is drawn at fair is because that's when a Customer is most likely to complain.

In reality, rather than complain, the average Customer who is unhappy will go somewhere else if there is an alternative. Some studies suggest that as many as 90 percent of unhappy Customers simply won't ever return to you; you'll never know what you did wrong, because they won't ever talk to you again. Worse, they will tell other people—lots of other people—how bad your service was.

The Headsets.com Way—Reinforcing the Customer Service Excellence Rating

The importance of the Customer Service Excellence Rating is abundantly clear whenever you visit their Customer Contact Center. Let's take a brief journey through the center in San Francisco.

- You exit the elevator, and you're greeted by the online Customer Service (OCS) team—three of the most efficient live-chat people I have ever met. Displayed beside them is a record of the team's performance to date for that week (individuals and the OCS Team), and proudly emblazoned in a large star is their current Customer Service Excellence Rating Today it's 16:1, which means the OCS Team, as a whole, provided excellent service to sixteen out of every seventeen Customers they have dealt with so far today.

- Entering the main section of the center, you see a large display of the various records held by members of the Headsets.com team. The highest weekly excellence rating for a team is 540:1, and it's currently held by two teams. There are also personal records, including the highest individual excellence rating, 156:1, and an individual OCS excellence record of 152:1.

- Once you enter the Customer Contact Center proper, you see a series of graphs that chart the company's overall performance for the past three years—both sales and Customer Service. Additionally there is a display of the company's past ten weeks of key metrics: excellence, attendance, sales, answer rate, and conversion rate.

- At the entrance to each pod (team area), performance figures for individuals and the team are clearly displayed as three key metrics: Customer Service Excellence, call conversion, and sales.

- Even the product support and credit approval teams proudly display their current excellence ratings. (Yes, even the credit approval teams are measured by their ability to provide Customer Love.)

- You round the corner and you're at the technical support team—the people who keep the place running (computers, telephones, etc.). They too have an excellence target that they aim to achieve for their internal Customers.

- Posted on the Customer Service Manager's door is a list of last week's highest performers, a tribute called the Triple Crown. These are the top three individuals in each of three categories: Customer Service Excellence, margin, and call conversion.

In addition to these public displays of gratitude and recognition are also weekly updates emailed to every member of the company, including consultants such as myself. These emails have both the highlights of the rating success for the previous week and praise for anyone who excelled. In the center, you can even see that praise being passed along between team members through pats on the back and "nice work last week," because everyone has bought in to the philosophy of Customer Love. All these people are Customers themselves—Customers with a capital C.

How about the other things that Headsets.com has identified as being important to their Customers?

Telephone Answer Rate

Based on discussions with their Customers, it was determined very early on that people like their calls to be answered by a real person and as quickly as possible. Although technology can help us reduce costs, it can also alienate Customers by depersonalizing the experience.

Sure, it would be possible to operate a Customer Contact Center using only voice mails and emails responded to on a daily or weekly basis. And yes, this would reduce costs. However, among all the workshops, seminars, and surveys that I've run, I have found only four people who would prefer the Customer Experience to be that way.

Do you think that it may have been purely coincidental that all four of those people worked for companies that provide technological solutions for Customer Contact? Call me jaded and cynical—I just can't bring myself to accept that they were a particularly reliable sample.

While we could convince ourselves that we could be more efficient by using voice recognition software, computer-controlled telephone queuing, and all sorts of gimmicks and gadgets designed to assist us or even to tell Customers that their call is "important," a basic desire for human beings is to be helped by other humans beings. Headsets.com promises that when a Customer calls, a real human being will answer within three rings.

Equally important is the OCS Team's commitment to answer every Customer's live chat within thirty seconds. In both cases, the teams achieve these exacting standards virtually all the time.

Response Times

These standards apply to all emails and messages (external and internal) that are left for anyone in the company. While a real person will answer every Customer within three rings, the specific person that the Customer may want to speak with may be helping another Customer. If that is the case and the Customer only wants to speak with that team member, a message is taken and immediately passed on to the person requested.

Every Customer that leaves a message for someone or sends an email is answered within two business hours. That's just the way it is!

Attendance and Punctuality Rates

Any company's operational criteria directly relates to their ability to provide service.

Staffing numbers per shift are designed to ensure that the maximum telephone coverage is available when Customers require it. Punctuality and the level of attendance is consequently critical in ensuring that Customers are dealt with efficiently, that their calls are answered by a real human being within three rings, and that the person who answers their call can talk with them for as long as they require without being pressured to take another call due to insufficient staffing.

Mike Faith's approach—and as he says, "It ain't rocket science"—has everyone who is supposed to be at work at work when they are supposed to be at work.

Call Conversion Rate

Headsets.com is not a charity, and part of their overall mission features responsibility to their investors and shareholders who would like them to make truckloads of money and who themselves are a type of Customer.

Without profit, Headsets.com couldn't continue to offer their Customers their very special type of Customer Love, let alone help teach the rest of the world what truly brilliant Customer Service is. To achieve this operational profit, a standard has been set for the number of calls that become either a sale or a new account. A new account simply constitutes obtaining that Customers' contact details so that next time they call, there is a record of what they wanted to know, the type of telephone they have, what advice they were given, and anything that is extra special about them (such as how to pronounce unusual names).

Here are the principles:

- They are given a seamless experience each time they call, regardless of which team member answers their call, because their Customer information is always readily at hand.

- The Customer can be updated on any special promotions or new products that the company may have at a later date.

Unlike many companies, who base their performance metrics solely on sales, the creation of a metric that combines new accounts with sales reduces the pressure to sell, sell, sell, and lets the team continue to put their Customers' needs first.

Shipping Accuracy

No matter how great the telephone or online service is, if a Customer receives the wrong product or receives a product later than it was promised, the overall Customer Experience will be pretty awful. So, the shipping teams target is 99.75 percent accuracy, and I can't remember the last time they missed it. Impressive, yes?

All of that being said, it's pretty much a matter of

- getting the numbers,
- setting the numbers,
- understanding the numbers,
- telling people about the numbers,
- improving the numbers
- and then *ignoring the numbers!*

This isn't quite as drastic, or as silly, as it sounds. What I mean by ignoring the numbers relates to something that Mike said to me very early in my time working with his team. Paraphrasing him, it went something like this:

While we spend a lot of time setting and monitoring our performance metrics, genuine Customer Love is about looking at the big picture, for both the company and the individual team members. They try to hit every Customer Love target; however, if for some reason someone has to choose between selling a headset and creating the best Customer Service Experience, the Customer must come first.

What Will I Do to Mention, Measure, Monitor, Motivate, and Manage?

a) Now—yes right away!

....

....

....

....

....

b) By the end of this week

....

....

....

....

....

c) By the end of this month

....

....

....

....

....

CHAPTER 7

Real Examples with a Capital A *(for Amazing)*

By this stage, you have a good grasp of the Customer-centric nature of Headsets.com's culture, of their style of Customer Love, and of what it means to give your Customers a capital C.

Now I'd like to illustrate this with a few real-life examples (I may have changed the names and details just a tad to simplify the examples).

Customer Love Example #1: Helping Everyone in Every Way You Can

I was sitting in with Cassandra, a member of the online Customer Service Team. She was simultaneously chatting with four or five Customers online through the Headsets. com's live person interface. That's a normal number of chats for this team: I've regularly seen David, Cassandra, and Didi happily running five or six simultaneous chats each. (Their ability to do this and to consistently achieve Customer Service Excellence ratings of 12:1 or more continues to amaze me.)

One of Cassandra's Customers had presented her with a particularly interesting request. He had recently purchased a Brand X PDA and was trying to convince it to do multiple tasks; he needed a specific type of adapter that was a nonstandard item. It was debatable whether such an adapter had ever been produced.

This became evident as Cassandra's chat continued and her Customer mentioned that Headsets.com was the fourth company that he'd approached. The first company he'd tried was the PDA manufacturer themselves, however he didn't really know what to ask for and he'd been thwarted by the multiple numeric prompts of their automated Customer Service system.

Undaunted, Cassandra spoke to Headsets.com's product support team and searched the web for clues—without losing a beat with any other Customers who had chatted in with their own requests. As the chat rate subsided and it became apparent that she would need to follow up with a few telephone calls for her PDA Customer, she asked for his contact number and if it would be okay for her to call him back within two hours, once she'd made a few more inquires for him. Her Customer loved this and enthusiastically replied, "You're incredible. That would be brilliant. Thank you so much."

David seamlessly took over Cassandra's two remaining chats, and she commenced phoning the PDA manufacturer directly. After struggling through several numeric prompts on the manufacturer's Customer Service system, she found her way through to a real person in their product team.

I was hearing only one side of this conversation, because I had been there to sit in and read Cassandra's live person chats, so you'll have to fill in the spaces yourself; it isn't hard to imagine the other side of this call.

Following is Cassandra's side of the conversation:

Hi, this is Cassandra from Headsets.com. I've got a Customer who has a Brand X PDA, and he's trying to find an adapter that will let two people use headsets from it at one time or a double headset that fits. Do you have anything like that?

Are you using a headset?

Is it corded or wireless?

There seems to be a buzz on it. Can you hear that at your end?

Yes, it does. Your volume is definitely low. How well can you hear me?

I'm sure that I can help you with that.

Would you like me to help you reset it? It won't take long?

From that point on, Cassandra identified the headset make and model for him, fixed the buzz and volume on his headset, set up a product support ticket for him so he could call Headsets.com any time he had an issue with one of his headsets (even though he hadn't bought the headsets from Headsets.com), *and* found a chain of stores that stocked the unique adapter that her PDA Customer had been trying to find.

Cassandra immediately tracked down the store nearest her PDA Customer and then called him back with the good news. The whole process had taken around fifteen minutes, so Cassandra had also significantly exceeded the two-hour expectation that she had set for her Customer.

Is it any wonder that he rated her live person chat as "excellent"?

Customer Love Example #2: Getting Back to Your Customer

There are always two ways of doing things: great and not so great.

First, the not so great. We've all experienced something like this: You call to report a fault with your cable TV, your telephone, or maybe your Internet connection. Your service provider runs some simple tests. They may even get you to do their work by running the tests for them.

Let's look at a simple fault that I experienced recently with my telephone line: I arrived home from a day of exhilarating meetings, a workshop, and coaching. My life definitely is exciting, challenging, and fun, so nothing strange so far.

I set about my routine of checking emails and voice mails— nothing of either. Now, this was strange.

I checked the modem, and a flashing light indicated that there was no DSL connection. I picked up my cordless headset—no dial tone. I tried my normal phone—no dial tone. I disconnected everything and tried a spare phone— still no dial tone.

I turned everything off, then on again—still nothing.

By then I was pretty sure that my landline was dead. I tracked down the telephone number for my telephone company and dialed them on my cell phone.

Step one—I was greeted by a "Please listen carefully to the options as these options have recently changed" message, soon followed by

> Press the number corresponding with the service you require:
>
> Press one for directory assistance.
>
> Press two for account inquiries.
>
> Press three if you are a Silver Service member.
>
> Press four if you are a Gold Service member.
>
> Press five if you are a Platinum Service member.
>
> Press six if you would like to report your service. [I'm still not quite sure why it was phrased like this—possibly their attempt at positive language.]
>
> Press seven if you are a small-business subscriber.
>
> Press eight if you are a special subscriber.
>
> Press nine or continue holding if you wish to speak with a service representative.

Press # if you wish to hear these options
again.

Of course, I had to press #, because by the time the list had
been completed, I'd forgotten which number would most
likely help me. I'd also been distracted by wondering what
the difference was between a gold and a platinum member,
thinking, *I'm a small business, and I'm special, aren't I?*

So, here we go again.

This time I found my way to option 6: "report your service."
I still wasn't exactly sure what that meant, however it
sounded like the best fit. After pressing button 6, I found
that I'd misheard their message, which was really "If you
would like to report a service difficulty."I really wasn't taking
much pleasure in reporting my service difficulty, however I
supposed some people may *like* doing it—some very, very
lonely people perhaps.

I thought, *Great! I'm through the menu.* Wrong! With the
benefit of hindsight, I should have gone for number 9,
although I had been trying to help them by going directly to
the right person—to someone who could help me because
he or she knew about service faults.

When I eventually did make my way through to the person
that was going to help me, my hero was voice recognition
software, which, naturally enough, didn't recognize my voice.
When I finally managed to simulate a computer recognizable
dialect I am asked for

- my telephone number,
- my company's name,

- my name,
- my address,
- my PIN,
- my date of birth, and
- my mother's maiden name.

By then I was expecting them to require my firstborn child before I could be put through to a real human being.

The simulated voice continues with "Are you calling from the telephone number with the fault?"

My reply: "Uh, no ... It doesn't work. That's why I'm calling."

"I'm sorry. I don't recognize that answer. ... Are you calling from the telephone number with the fault?"

"No," I replied.

At last, the computer officially gave me recognition with this: "Thank you for calling, Mr. Welsh. To assist us in identifying your fault, could you please follow the following steps?"

Two thoughts immediately crossed my mind, other than "I need a new telephone company":

> Thought 1: Follow the following steps?! Couldn't they have found a better way of saying that? What else could I do, run ahead of them? Give them to a friend as a birthday present, perhaps?

Thought 2: Now they want me to do their work for them.

For the next five minutes, I ran a series of simple tests for my telephone company only to be told by the computer, "At this time, we cannot diagnose your fault. You will be transferred to a service representative immediately."

A brief, high-pitched tone followed as I was transferred to "You have been answered by (name withheld to protect the not-so-innocent)'s automated answering service. We are currently experiencing unusual levels of delay. Your call is important to us. Your call has been placed in a queue and will be answered in the order received, by the next available operator. ... Due to the current level of delay, you may choose to call back at another time." Cue the mournful Muzak.

I won't burden you with the lengthy interrogation that I received when I was eventually transferred to an offshore call center. Needless to say, the experience wasn't a happy one for me.

And then, after the technical services representative had exhausted all of his knowledge, it was time to arrange a service visit to my house. *Great*, I thought. "What time?" I foolishly asked.

"The technician will be there sometime between eight a.m. and noon tomorrow."

"Can we lock in a more precise time, because I will need to stay home from my office to do this?" I asked.

"No, Mr. Welsh. I can only book service visits for morning or afternoon, nothing more than that. But I can ask them to call you at eleven thirty if they won't make it to you by noon."

Well, they'd clearly set expectations—including an expectation that I probably wouldn't have telephone or Internet connections for two or three days.

Now the Headsets.com way.

An important aspect of giving your Customers a capital C is setting very clear expectations for your Customers and then exceeding them. These need to be reasonable expectations that show them they are important to you.

Let's say a Headsets.com team member doesn't have an immediate answer to a challenging question. Perhaps the Customer has an unusual cell phone needing a special adapter to use a hands-free speaker system. A solution to this may require some research to determine the best possible device. Rather than keep their Customer on the line for ten or fifteen minutes, they commit to calling them back within two hours. They'll confirm the most convenient time and number for their Customer to be contacted.

They find out the answer and call their Customer back; either before the two hours is up or precisely at the time specified by their Customer—whichever is more convenient to their Customer. If Headsets.com doesn't stock the necessary item, they'll be able to tell their Customer at least one or two places he or she could try.

Similarly, I've heard the Headsets.com product support team say something like this: "Either of those adapters will work with your phone. How about I send you both on a free trial. That way you see which one you like the best, and then you can send the other one back when you're ready."

Customer Love Example #3: Empowering Your Team

Another significant difference between Headsets.com and many other companies is the manner in which it empowers all of its team to assist their Customers.

As with most companies, the managers have the ability to act immediately on anything that can improve their Customers' experience; in Headsets.com this empowerment extends throughout the company.

So that you can understand this better, I'd like to explain the company's structure a little more.

The Core Customer Service Team is divided into a number of smaller teams called pods. Each pod is supervised by a Captain who in turn is a member of the Captains Team, which is accountable to the Customer Service Manager. While the captains are always available to make decisions on exemptions, exceptions and special cases, it is very rare that a Customer wants to escalate a call. This is because pod members have a high degree of delegated authority to do whatever it takes to ensure the best possible Customer Experience.

For example, I've often heard the following type of conversations when our new hires are in training. (Of course, once their initial training has been completed, they know the answer without asking. Well, most of the time anyway.)

> NEW HIRE: My Customer, Julie, has lost an ear bud, and she is concerned that she can't use her headset until she gets a new pair. She's been with us for a few years. Can I send them overnight? She's really nice.

> CAPTAIN: What would you like if you were her?

> NEW HIRE: Free overnight! Done!

Customer Love Example #4: Responsibility and Accountability

A key principle at Headsets.com is that everyone is both responsible and accountable. While this may seem like a case of overenthusiastic semantics, because common usage has made responsibility and accountability virtually synonymous, there is a difference between the two—particularly in relation to Headsets.com.

Responsibility means that everyone accepts the responsibility to help Customers and to create the best possible experience for them. By its nature, this responsibility means that they *respond* to their Customers' needs, wants, and desires.

Accountability means that all employees are answerable for the level of success they achieve in creating an experience of Customer Service Excellence while maintaining their individual (and the company's) integrity. Their accountability is to their Customers, managers, captains, and the team as a whole.

Everyone at Headsets.com holds each other accountable, not only for the direct Customer Service Experience, for the indirect experience as well.

The indirect experience includes the total operation of Headsets.com and is illustrated on a daily basis in what are called huddles. These are regular gatherings that include various members of the Headsets.com team. One huddle may be the Core Customer Service captains; another may include managers, shipping, and technical support; while yet others may be the members of a pod.

During huddles, each person holds others, and themselves, accountable for their actions, including me as an external coach.

If, during a huddle, I state that the most important thing that I am going to do that day is to coach five people, however someone in the huddle feels that goal may not be realistic or may not be the most important thing that I should be doing for the company that day, her or she will ask about it.

Additionally, if I set that target on Tuesday (whether queried of not), and I haven't achieved it by the time of the next huddle, I will be held accountable to explain why I didn't achieve it and how I was going to rectify the situation.

This rule of accountability applies uniformly across the company. I've heard members of the technical support team held accountable for missing their software update target on the same day that the CEO was asked why he hadn't achieved his goal for the previous day.

Individuals are held accountable for any instance that they do not achieve the best possible Customer Experience, and every member of the team feels the responsibility to maintain both their own and the company-wide Customer Service Excellence standards.

On the rare occasion that the company-wide Customer Service Excellence rate or the call answer rate has slipped, even marginally, below the standard, the center buzzes with activity as everyone puts in that extra bit of effort to ensure that their Customers feel loved. The energy lifts, and people talk with increased focus. Captains work with their teams, their Customer Service Manager, and their Coaches. And the Contact Center Managers are on the floor, talking with people, helping motivate them. Everyone, without fail, pulls together.

Though they know they are responsible and will be held accountable, their true drive is a genuine love for what they do.

Customer Love Example #5:
The Reciprocal Effect

Customer Love isn't a one-way street: as well as creating Customer Loyalty, word of mouth is the most cost-effective marketing tool that any company can have.

Numerous studies have examined the flow-on effects of the Customer Experience, and it is generally accepted that a great Customer Service Experience results in that individual Customer telling nine or more people about it.

The power of a personal recommendation should never be underestimated. All of my clients—every company or individual that I coach—came to me through the good word of one of my existing clients. I never advertise; my website is simply an information source. The first time new clients approach me, I ask them who referred them and offer to visit them to see if we are a good fit for each other.

Consequently, we are almost always a good fit because my referring client knows what I'm like, what I do, and how I do it. They wouldn't have put the two of us together if we weren't a good fit.

While the Headsets.com team is a Customer of mine, I too am a Customer of theirs. On numerous occasions, I've been on the receiving end of Customer Love: from introducing me to prospective new clients to giving me a new headset to generally making me feel like part of the Headsets.com family.

In return, I might find myself in San Francisco with a few spare days, so I call into the office and coach people in my spare time—free of charge—or maybe I throw in a free weekend workshop or two.

So, just as they help set their Customers' expectations and then exceed them, I help set their expectations of me and then try to exceed them.

It's definitely a case of what goes around comes around with Customer Love. If you like, it's karma with a capital K.

Customer Love Example #6:
The Follow-Through

Another aspect of helping your Customers realize that they are important enough to warrant a capital C is the way you follow-through with them—whether it's expected or not.

Recently I was live listening with Eric, from the product support team, when out of the blue he called a Customer, "Sandra," just because he had a spare moment.

Eric had previously worked with Sandra on an unusually challenging microphone configuration. There was a pulsing tone heard by people that she spoke to using her headset. Sandra and Eric had tried a number of different settings and positions, and still the tone occurred. The pulsing was an intermittent concern and so increased the challenge to isolate its source.

Eric had sent her a replacement headset four days before, and from previous experience he knew she was less technically savvy than some. Hence this "spare time call":

ERIC: Hi, Sandra, This is Eric from Headsets.com. I'm calling to check that you received your new headset and it's working for you.

SANDRA: Ah, hi, Eric. Yes, I have it. However I ... I'm ... well, I'm not sure how to connect it. I know there are instructions; however they're, well, a bit hard to understand.

ERIC: That's perfectly fine, Sandra. That's what I'm here for. Let's get your headset connected and working for you.

Eric had made her day. Once it was connected, he ran a quick check to confirm that all was working and that the previous pulsing tone was no longer evident.

Making that call wasn't something specified in the training manual or on a checklist; it was simply by Eric's initiative. And it's an illustration of how much he cares about his Customers.

Eric wasn't seeking kudos for it. This is a simple example of the follow-through Customer Love that goes on daily at Headsets.com.

By the way, I later heard a recorded call of Eric's. He'd called Sandra again to check on her new headset.

This wasn't a one-off. I've often heard our product support and Core Customer Service Team members follow-through like this as a "spare time" activity, even if the spare time is outside their normal working hours.

Customer Love Example #7: What We Can Do for You

Another great aspect of the company's culture is that everyone buys into it. As I mentioned earlier, Customers come first, and when calls are coming in, the companywide priority is to answer them. Rather than having calls in a queue, managers, trainers, and even the CFO answer calls if their Customers need them too.

On a busy day such as this, Art, the credit approval manager, took an inbound Core Customer Service call rather than having a Customer wait. "Mary" had an older, out-of-production version of a headset that used a cord to connect it to a wireless belt pack. After many years of use, it had simply worn out. While the cord could be disconnected if you tried very hard to do it, it was considered part of the headset and couldn't be purchased separately. As Mary's headset and belt pack were still in good working order, she preferred not to buy a completely new headset solution if she could avoid the expense.

Art checked to see what could be done. Headsets.com didn't stock the cord separately, although we did have a couple of new headset systems still in stock

Art recognized that Mary was price conscious and wanted to see what he could do to help her. He asked if he could call her back in two hours, and she agreed. Art immediately rang our shipping team.

Within ten minutes, a call came back from shipping. Sure enough, tucked away on the returns shelf was that headset, cord intact. They removed the cord, and voilà: Mary's solution. The thing is, Headsets.com sells new headsets, and technically this one was used.

Art called Mary back immediately.

> ART: Hi, Mary, this is Art from Headsets.com. I'm calling about your replacement headset cord.

> MARY: Thank you so much for calling back, Art. Have you done any good?

Art explained the situation and how we'd
tracked down a used cord for her, and of
course that we only sell new products.

So—

ART: Mary, how much do you feel that the cord is worth?

MARY: Oh, I guess ten dollars or so.

ART: Great. I'll send your cord to you, and next time you
have a chance, you can donate that ten dollars to your
favorite charity. I'll have your cord with you in three
days. Is there anything else I can help you with today?

Mary then simply gushed with excitement, enthusiasm, and
gratitude at the amazing service she'd just received and
what Headsets.com could do, rather than what they couldn't.

Customer Love Example #8:
Exceeding Your Reputation

The examples above show several aspects of Customers
being important enough to have a capital C:

- how your reputation can precede you and what it can
  mean when you live up to it;

- how, even if you may not know the answer, you
  know that you have a support team behind you and
  someone will;

- how important it is to always accept the challenge
  and, corny as it may sound, to grow from it (both you
  and your company).

Nick and Scott, our technical support team, do an incredible job of keeping the company's technology running smoothly. They're basically on call 24/7 and respond immediately to any concern. Still, they do like to have downtime occasionally, such as a moment or two with friends.

On one particular day, Nick had arranged to have dinner with a friend who worked in a corporate HQ in downtown San Francisco. He rolled up to meet a friend, Don, at his office to grab a quick drink after work and then to catch up over dinner. As Nick introduced himself to the receptionist, her ears perked up. She introduced herself as Marcia and then quickly added, "You're from Headsets.com, aren't you?"

No sooner had Nick confirmed this than she began showing him her wireless headset and telling him about the buzz she was hearing. Nick looked at it briefly, and while he's brilliant with telephones and computers, wireless headsets aren't his forte. However, rather than admit defeat, he immediately called our product support team and introduced the receptionist to JD, product support captain. Within a minute or two, JD had resynchronized her headset, and she was back on the air.

She hadn't purchased her headset from Headsets.com, however she was a headset user and she needed help, so she was helped.

Ultimately several people from that company were helped over the next hour or two. Apparently they'd been experiencing buzzes and volume challenges for months, and because their headsets were out of warrantee, they'd decided to simply put up with the inconvenience. Now, at last, they'd found someone who would help them.

You can lay odds that next time they buy headsets, the people that cared and helped them will be the first people they call. (In fact, they even said as much to Nick the next time that he had drinks with them.)

Nick told this story at a huddle, praising JD. He was totally unaware that JD had told the same story at a different huddle praising *him*. (JD and I were the only people participating in both huddles).*And* Nick and JD compared notes so that Nick knew what had been done to improve that company's headsets performance.

You see, at Headsets.com, applying a capital C isn't restricted to existing Customers; they apply it to anyone who needs help with a headset. Product support is offered free for life—yours, not your headset's.

Every day, dozens of amazing Customer Experiences occur at Headsets.com. Obviously there must be hundreds that go by unnoticed because, as Dave, the training manager, put it recently, "Well, this is what we do."

A key challenge will always be finding new ways to raise the stakes and keep exceeding the expectations of your Customers. However, like Headsets.com, you'll soon find that it's amazing what you can achieve when you really set your mind to it.

What does this mean to you?

The examples in this chapter are simply starting points for your imagination and ingenuity. Every time you find a new way to amaze your Customers, you add to your power of attraction—by attracting new Customers and maintaining the loyalty of your existing Customers through your Customer-centric culture and language. What it will mean to you is a friendlier, more energetic environment, a happier, healthier team and Customer base, and ultimately a better bottom line.

What Will I Do to Recognize Examples of Great Customer-Centric Service among My Own Team?

a) Now—yes right away!

....
....
....
....
....

b) By the end of this week

....
....
....
....
....

c) By the end of this month

....
....
....
....
....

CHAPTER 8

Promises with a Capital T *(for Trust)*

All great relationships have a solid foundation of trust to build on, and Customer relationships are exactly the same. Every time we deal with a Customer, the first psychological need that exists is the need for reassurance; reassurance that they

- have dialed the correct number;
- have reached someone in the company that can really help them;
- have reached a person who isn't too busy to help them and that cares about them;
- haven't done something "silly" or "dumb"; and
- have reached someone who won't make them feel that way if they have.

By nature, we human beings are insecure animals. So how do we ensure that our Customers feel secure with us?

There are four basic rules that can help us with this:

- Make promises and keep them. There are no exceptions to this, internally or externally.

- Be visible. This means being accessible and accountable to all your Customers.

- Be consistent. Be uniformly, continuously, obviously, and openly consistent in everything you do and with everyone.

- Mind your language. Use language that reassures your Customers that they and their needs are important to you.

Let's explore these "rules" in more detail.

Make Promises and Keep Them

As an integral part of being responsible and accountable, everyone in the company believes in making commitments—promises, if you like. In this respect, there are two critical things that differentiate Headsets.com from many other companies.

First, everyone at Headsets.com is prepared and encouraged to make commitments to their Customers. Second, they are empowered to do what is necessary to meet these commitments. More than that—they are held accountable if they don't meet their commitments.

One of the reasons many people shy away from making clear commitments to their Customers is because once you make a commitment, you have set your Customers' expectations. And if you don't deliver, your Customers may try to hold you accountable.

And so they should!

Rather than this meaning "don't make commitments," it means that you readily make them and meet them.

As an adjunct to making commitments to your Customers, if your Customers are genuinely important enough to warrant a capital C, they are equally important enough to give them clear expectations about what you are going to do for them, how you will do it, and when you will do it. And then, if you possibly can, exceed those expectations.

If you say you'll find out what the product number is, and it turns out to be a product that you don't stock, you find the product number and then find out where your Customer can get that part.

Another key aspect of building trust through commitment is the open accountability that goes hand-in-hand with telling your Customer your name and telephone extension. At Headsets.com, whenever team members answer the telephone, they thank the Customer for calling and tell the Customer their name. If there is any follow-up required or it seems that their Customer may want to call back at another time for more information, the team members always repeat their own name and provide their Customer with their telephone extension.

This is what making a commitment to your Customers is all about: taking responsibility for your Customers, letting them know that they are entitled to hold you accountable for the commitment that you've made to them, and in so doing, ensuring that your Customer has confidence in you and your company.

The Headsets.com Way—Making Promises

In previous examples, I've shown how Headsets.com makes commitments to their Customers and how they set, meet, and exceed their Customers' expectations by making and keeping promises.

They also openly help to set Customer expectations by prolifically publishing a set of promises, known as The Promises. These promises are included on the website, in every catalog that is sent out, and in virtually every Customer document that the company produces.

The Promises

- **Satisfaction Guaranteed**

  Our 60-Day Unconditional Money Back Guarantee means that if for any reason *(or no reason)* you're not absolutely delighted with your purchase from Headsets.com, you may exchange for any other product you'd prefer to try, or you may return the products and receive a prompt and courteous refund, no questions asked.

- **Compatibility Guaranteed**

  Our headsets are compatible with 98% of phones: as specialists, we know what works. In the rare event that we supply a headset that is incompatible with your phone, you'll receive a refund and we'll send you a FREE return shipping label.

Your phone call will be answered by a live person, based in San Francisco, who is eager to help. It's our goal to answer all calls in four rings, however if we can't take your call right away we promise to call you back within two business hours. If you click on 'Instant Live Chat' at our website you'll receive a live response within 60 seconds.

- **Full Replacement**

  All products carry a one-year full replacement product warranty, and corded office telephone headsets and amplifiers carry a two-year full replacement product warranty. We'll replace any faulty product without hesitation, so you know that you'll never have to wait for a repair.

- **Free Lifetime Product Support**

  It should only take a few minutes to unpack your new headsets, connect them, and make your first call. You're welcome to make that first call to Headsets.com. We'll gladly help you to fine tune the volume controls so you speak and hear with crystal clarity. Our headset specialists are on call at 1-800-432-3738 Mon.—Fri. 6:00am—4:30pm PST.

- **Management Accountability**

  We promise you efficient and friendly service at all times. If you're not satisfied, neither are we. Our managers are available to address any concerns:

- **Tootsie Rolls**

  Yes, in every package!

Every member of the Headsets.com team knows these verbatim. Especially the Tootsie Rolls. Yes, they really do include free Tootsie Rolls with every order.

To me, including the Tootsie Rolls in their promises to their Customers says a lot about their company and Customer Service—primarily that life doesn't always have to be serious!

Remember that your Customers and your team are human, and we all like to have fun sometimes. (Remember what I said about the *Virgin* brand at the start of this book?)

Being Visible

Many companies confuse transparency with visibility. They believe that transparency requires that actions, functions, and decision-making processes are discernable. Some consider transparency to simply be an openness or accessibility of management to staff, while others believe they have achieved transparency when everyone they want to know about them knows about them.

All of these are great in their own way and are essential in modern business. Headsets.com does have these types of transparency, accessibility, and accountability, however also what they call "visibility," which means their key people being visible, and accessible, to their Customers.

The Headsets.com Way—Visibility

An important element of The Promises is management accountability. To back this up, they openly publish the names and direct telephone numbers for their

- President/CEO,

- Customer Service Manager, and

- Shipping Manager.

Between these three people, any Customer can have concerns quickly resolved with no need to fill out forms or to be shuffled among numerous other people first. If a Customer calls these numbers, they will go straight through to someone who has the ability to help them.

If for any reason Customers calls the 1(800)HEADSETS number and ask to be transferred to any of these three people, there is a no-questions-asked approach. They are immediately transferred to that person. If that person is helping another Customer at the time, a message can be left and will be responded to within two business hours.

In reality, due to the company's culture and its approach to Customer Service, very rarely do these people receive such negative calls. As Courtney Wight once told me, "One of the nice things about having my number readily available is that Customers call me with compliments and praise."

The company's approach of visibility includes the use of their team members' real names, and if two people have the same first name, they find a way of clearly identifying each other to their Customers. For instance, Josh is a long-standing product support team member, and a team captain's name is also Josh, so he's referred to by his initials, JD, to prevent confusion and maintain visibility and accountability for Customers.

In addition to this, Customers can see what each team member looks like, because their photos are included on the website, wearing their favorite headset, of course.

Ensure Consistency

We've already discussed the way Headsets.com has created its own set of metrics and how it measures, monitors, and modifies them to ensure that its high standards are maintained. However, another intrinsic aspect of their secret to achieving consistency is through their training.

To quote Mike Faith: "We have our very best train the rest to be the best."

What better way to both pass on ability and knowledge and to retain your star performers than to encourage them to train others. While some may not be natural trainers, and you may need to nurture them. By giving them the opportunity to train their peers, you can

- reinforce the profile of Customer Service as a career within your company;

- be available to recognize and reward high performance in more than merely monetary ways;

- pass on valuable knowledge to your new hires;

- encourage others to improve their performance with a goal of becoming trainers themselves; and

- add to the skill set of your team by encouraging people who actively deal with your in-coming Customers to train your In-ternal Customers.

This also means that you can pass on some of those absolute gems that these people do to naturally, instinctively, and continually develop your Customer Experience with every new group of people that is trained.

Remember too that your trainers will learn from every new hire they train.

The Headsets.com Way—
Using the Best to Train the Best

Headsets.com's star performers can, if they choose, help further develop the Customer Experience by

- becoming genuine trainers who run specific training classes with new hires;

- mentoring new hires during their first two to six weeks;

- providing more advanced, topic-based training;

- providing one-off or a short series of presentations in the regular Thursday meetings; and/or

> •   creating and distributing briefing notes on specific products, topics, and styles of helping our Customer.

Mind Your Language

Where would a promise be without the words—the right words, the absolute best words—to ensure the best results.

This is especially the case with telephone- and Internet-based companies like Headsets.com. That's what originally led Mike to me. Yes, I'm a voice coach. I deal with the way people sound: the tone and rhythm of their voice and how clearly they speak. I also deal with the bigger picture—the total package of the voice, which includes the words we use; how we tailor our message to suit the ear (and mind) of the person we are delivering it to; and the context within which we deliver it.

My work is largely experiential psychology (with a dash of neuro-psychology) based on an understanding of the interface between language and emotions.

Let's have a look at the language that helps your Customers have a capital C.

We've all heard about positive language, and yes, it is important—very important. I'd be surprised if you haven't tried to use the power of positive language at some time or another.

However, at Headsets.com I've been given carte blanche to explore positive language as far as I possibly can, and I've been supported in every way. Consequently, they have now taken what was common business sense (that is, using positive, friendly, professional language) and made it an art form.

The Headsets.com Way—Minding Your Language

Welcoming language—Put yourself in your Customer's place. How great is it when someone greets you with a smile and a thank-you? How incredible is it when someone signs off with another thank-you and a heartfelt "Have a great day" or something similar? The key is to be genuinely friendly, welcoming your Customers and helping them to feel appreciated. At Headsets.com, there are no specific phrases that must be used. The principles are the important part. It needs to genuinely come from you as an individual. Spread your energy and enthusiasm; it's contagious.

Smile—You'll hear every expert say it again and again, and there's a simple reason that we say it: it's true! Your Customers can hear your smile in your voice, so do it, and keep doing it. It really does help!

Positive words—While we all know that this is important, it can still be one of the most challenging steps to take and may take time to master. It requires you to replace negative or neutral (noncommittal) words like *uh-huh, okay, all right,* and *mhhm,* and even phrases like *don't forget* and *no problem,* with words like *absolutely, perfect, great, wonderful, excellent,* and *definitely.*

A specific example of the Headsets.com approach is the adage "No problem is a problem."We suggest that "No problem" and "Not a problem" infer that there could have been a problem, though you're prepared to ignore it now. While on the surface it can seem positive, it can plant a negative seed in your Customer's mind. (That is, it really could be a problem; however I'll magnanimously let you off this time!)

Another example of this high level of positive, reinforcing language is the way we remind people to "remember" rather than asking them "not to forget."

Can-do phrases—To create the most positive experience, everyone at Headsets.com makes a point of telling their Customers what they can do for them rather than what they can't. One of the most annoying words in the English language, particularly from a Customer's point of view, is *no*, and one of the most pleasant can be *yes*.

It's easy to say no, however it takes time and practice to learn how to say yes to a question you would normally, instinctively answer with a no. However, the impact on your Customers' feelings is well worth the effort on your part.

While I've already mentioned this concept as a key Headsets.com communication principle, you should also be aware that a rule also applies that will affect the way that you use your can-do phrases: always tell your Customers the truth.

Offer your Customers an extra chance to ask a question—Always remember to ask our Customers if there's anything else we can do for them, because there often is. Sometimes it might even be buying something additional from you.

Always hang up last—This is something that you will notice without fail at Headsets.com: no one hangs up while a Customer is still on the line. One of the most annoying and frustrating sounds that I've ever heard is the telephone being hung up just as I've thought of that "other thing" I'd wanted to ask.

Be real—While it is essential that you and everyone in your company practice these techniques, it's just as important that everyone takes genuine ownership and personalizes them until they become part of their everyday life.

Finally, of course, there's this:

Customers with a capital C—Recognize the proper nouns; that's what this book is all about: creating a Customer Service Culture where the Customer is always recognized as someone important enough to warrant a capital C.

Capitalization helps achieve Customer Service Excellence through language in several ways. Its use is not the norm: the capital will make the words stand out in any sentence. Consequently, people will notice and think about it—both consciously and unconsciously. Its impact has several features:

- The words stand out in documents, and this prompts us to think about them and why they are so important.

- Checking and rechecking documents for the capitalization of *Customer* helps to reinforce the importance of this word in our team's minds, because they are prepared to spend time and energy to ensure that they are consistently capitalized—and time is money. So the mental link here is that the company wouldn't spend money on something that isn't important.

- When our Customers see the capitalization for the first time, they may ask about it. This is a perfect opportunity to show them how important they are to us.

- Once our Customers know the reason behind our use of capitalization, every time they read one of our documents they're reminded how important they are to us, consciously and subconsciously.

All of these techniques definitely help make people feel special, and if that isn't worth doing, I don't know what is!

The training opportunities referred to above are the most common approaches to training within the company; however, training initiatives are limited only by your imagination. The Headsets.com management team will consider virtually any suggestions and generally is prepared to at least give them a try.

While many of the techniques referred to in this chapter may be reasonably well known, it is their consistent use and development as a comprehensive package that ultimately leads to the success of a Headsets.com style of Customer Experience.

What Will I Do to Ensure That We Make and Fulfill All Our Promises to All Our Customers?

a) Now—yes right away!

....

....

....

....

....

b) By the end of this week

....

....

....

....

....

c) By the end of this month

....

....

....

....

....

CHAPTER 9

Patience with a Capital T *(for Time)*

L ike all good things, greatness comes to those who are prepared to work, wait, and then work some more.

Headsets.com didn't develop their approach overnight: it's taken them ten years, and it's still evolving.

By permitting me to write this book, Headsets.com has given you the advantage of their learning experience over the past decade. While you will have the ability to use its principles to improve your Customer Service, you will of course need to adapt them to suit your own unique circumstances and your equally unique Customers. While you do, Headsets.com will continue to grow, develop, and evolved their techniques, as they always have.

Every time I work with Headsets.com I see new and exciting things integrated into their Customer Experience.

Even while I'm working with them over the phone, from wherever I am in the world, we're exploring new ideas: finding new ways to help Customers and personalizing each experience, internal and external.

Clearly it takes time to create a world-class benchmark for Customer Service Excellence, and your quest to improve should be unceasing.

It is also essential to let your Customers be involved in dictating the pace. Spending a few extra seconds with each and every Customer will improve your Customers' experience by

- helping them know that they are important to you;
- letting them feel more in control of the situation;
- increasing their trust in you and loyalty to your company;
- permitting their expectations to be appropriately set;
- helping them feel that they have been listened to;
- providing you with an opportunity to learn from them with every new experience.

This applies both to the big picture of evolving your Customer Service Culture and to the smaller, yet equally important, picture of each individual Customer interaction.

How do you ensure that you give your Customers all the time they need? Avoid rushing them, ask simple questions to prompt their thoughts, listen to them and let them talk, reassure them, relax them and always ask if there's anything else you can do for them.

You've come this far, so now let's look at some of the extra things you can do. While they are time-consuming, they will make a difference. And remember, "Death really is in the details."

> ### The Headsets.com Way—
> ### Giving Your Customers Time
>
> While Headsets.com has established a number of metrics to help them gauge the success of individuals and their teams as a whole, these do not include metrics that set either a minimum number of Customers that they need to deal with each day or a maximum call duration. In fact, quite the opposite applies: on several occasions, I've been asked by captains to coach individual team members who they feel are handling too many call per day.
>
> My work with these people has been to help them bond with their Customers and to read their Customers' needs. If they are busy Customers, we definitely want to help them as quickly and as efficiently as possible; however, care needs to be taken to ensure that we assess each Customer's needs and not generalize our approach to calls by carrying one Customer's needs into another Customer's call (that is, treat each Customer as an individual with a unique set of needs, wants, and desires and conduct your call appropriately). Spend as much time with your Customers as they want you to, and always leave them feeling that they enjoyed your personalized, professional, and friendly service.

Truly Respect Your Customers

This may sound like both a given and a cliché. However, it is also something that Headsets.com takes to a new level.

In some places that I've worked, I've been surrounded by posters that proclaim how important their Customers are and that they must always be respected.

"The Customer Is Always Right"

"Consumers Are Numbers—Customers Are People"

"Be everywhere, do everything, and never
fail to astonish the Customer"

My question to each of these organizations was, "Do you really mean it? Do you truly respect and care about your Customers?"

Respect is much more that merely mouthing a series of quotes and drilling your team on scripts designed to make Customers feel good. The very nature of "making" anyone do anything is anathema to respect, and if the words don't come from the heart, you can do more damage than good.

Hand in hand with respect goes sincerity. If you don't really feel it, you can't consistently give it. Headsets.com has made an art form of Customer Respect. After all, how much more respect can you have than to give them a capital C?

However, it can take time for someone new to the concept to fully understand and adopt this type of culture.

The Headsets.com Way—
Respecting Your Customers

At Headsets.com, Customer Respect starts on day 1 of training. From that point on, you will be held accountable if you ever disrespect a Customer.

At Headsets.com, we respect our Customers in the following ways:

- Letting them speak. We aim for a 70:30 ratio—that is, 70 percent of the time we listen and 30 percent we speak.

- Speaking with them rather than talking to them. This may seem like semantics, however the result is that, even when a Customer has a gap in knowledge, he or she never feels inadequate, patronized, or talked down to.

- Using language that reassures them that we understand them and we will do our best to help them.

- Using language that shows friendliness combined with professionalism.

- Assisting them to understand, rather than correcting them.

- Always telling the truth, although occasionally we may need to soften the blow a little.

The language used in marketing and promotions by Headsets. com is also intrinsically respectful to our Customers. While the marketing of many companies is run by cynical advertising executives who treat their target audience as sheep, virtually everyone in the company has come up through the ranks and been trained in giving Customers respect. In fact, Chris, the head of marketing was previously the Customer Service Manager for our Contact Center.

Customer respect extends to after a call as well. Even if we have an uncomfortable or challenging call with a Customer who has carried emotional baggage from a previous situation into our call, we never discuss it in the work environment.

While no Customer will ever be discussed negatively, on the rare occasion that team members experience calls "rattle" them, they may approach their captain or me with "Hi, I just need to talk through this. Have you got a minute?" They will then talk through it in privacy so that

- they feel better and can keep helping their Customers without it affecting future calls, and

- they can find new ways to deal with challenging situations.

One of the wonderful things about working for Headsets.com is that the overall approach to Customer Service means that such situations are extremely rare. In my time with Headsets. com, I have had less than a dozen such conversations with team members. That's pretty remarkable given that each Core Customer Service Team member deals with in excess of ten thousand Customer calls per year.

More on Respect—Correcting the Incorrect

Earlier I mentioned the adage "The Customer is always right." This isn't one of my favorite sayings, though I do commend the merit behind it. While I may feel that the Customer needn't necessarily always be right, I do know that with true Customer Respect, he or she is never wrong. (Another valuable lesson I learnt from Mike Faith.)

In our day-to-day life, one way to gauge respect is by examining the manner in which we correct someone. You'll often observe people power-tripping as they correct others, expounding their knowledge for all the world to hear and in turn belittling the other person. Often this is not a conscious activity; it is merely humans doing what we do best: being human. Most of us are insecure by nature, and we take any opportunity to improve our esteem or status, even at the expense of someone else. More often than not, this comes across as being disrespectful.

Consequently one of the most sensitive times in a Customer Service relationship is when the Customer doesn't quite have the most accurate information or perspective.

The Headsets.com Way—
Helping a Customer to Fully Understand

Should situations arise where a Headsets.com Customers are incorrect, they will always be treated with respect and given as much help as possible to understand any additional information that they may need in order to have the most accurate view of the situation.

For instance, if a Customer calls and asks specifically for a headset that is incompatible with a certain telephone system, the team member who speaks with him or her will explain the compatibility concerns and will recommend an alternative (even if it is less expensive).

If a Customer continues to insist on a specific headset, even after the compatibility concern has been explained, we' send our Customer the headset of their dreams, making a note in their account file about the compatibility concerns and ensuring that the headset is either placed on a trial or sent to our Customer with a reminder that there is a sixty-day, no-questions-asked, money-back guarantee.

> I've even known our people to call such Customers a week
> or so after they have received the headset to see if it's
> working out.

Putting Yourself in Your Customers' Place

It's essential that you know and understand the complete
Customer Experience. This is sometimes done through
what is called "mystery shopping." While you can employ
companies that specialize in this, you can—and I think
should—also try it for yourself.

It's simple enough. Call your contact center; chat online;
use your website; go into a store; read your own catalogs,
brochures, and advertising; watch your television
commercials—find every way that your Customers and
potential Customers experience you—and experience it for
yourself.

Take notes about

- your overall impression,
- how you were treated,
- how long it took,
- how easy it was, and
- anything else that you feel could be relevant.

I specifically use the word *feel* because this is about emotions,
impressions, and perceptions as much as numbers.

Have your team members buy something from your company and ask themselves, "Would I buy that again from me?" And get people whose judgment you respect to do the same thing.

Next, do exactly the same thing with someone who sells what you sell, and ask yourself the same question again, adding, "If I'm being honest, who would I buy from me or them?"

Once you've shopped your types of products, there's still more shopping you can do. Just because you sell shoes or bubble gum or refrigerator doesn't mean you can't learn from someone who sells something else. After all, you're reading this book about a company that sells headsets so that you can learn from them, so go out and experience Customer Service on every level and see what you can adapt for your own purposes.

An aside: I'm currently working on helping a hospital team become more hospitable by applying techniques originally developed for hotels and restaurants. My value as a coach isn't because I know one industry and stick to that industry; it's because I have a broad background and am happy to borrow from every industry that I've ever been involved with. I readily and productively adapted their approaches, activities, and ideas to every other industry that I'm now involved with.

What Next?

Do as Headsets.com does.

Once you've tried everything we've explored in this book and hopefully have some new ideas that this book has stimulated you to explore, go right back to the beginning.

In order to stay ahead of the game, you cannot afford to sit on your laurels. Remember that a laurel bush has thorns, so imagine what you'll get if you simply sit on yours.

Go out there and make your mark. Be recognized as a company on its way to becoming the best at what you do. Then jump right back into the driver's seat; keep track of your Customers' changing wants, needs, and desires; stay informed about what everyone else in Customer Service is doing; and take what you're doing even further.

Then it's back to *mention, measure, monitor, motivate, and manage*. Train, retrain, and explore every avenue at your disposal to exceed your Customers' expectations continually.

And always remember to help your Customers know that they are important enough to be your

Customer with a capital C.

The skill set developed with Headsets.com and described throughout this book opens the door for you to develop your own unique style, your own Customer Love. We've simply shown you Customer Love the Headsets.com way! It isn't a fool-proof system—not every aspect will work for every company every time, however this package has worked extremely well for this one, mid-sized US company. A company I highly recommened you explore further if you genuinely care about your Customers.

What Will I Do Ensure That Our Customers Always Have a Capital C?

a) Now—yes right away!

....

....

....

....

....

b) By the end of this week

....

....

....

....

....

c) By the end of this month

....

....

....

....

....

Author's Final Note

(As if any author ever has a final word.)

Since I commenced writing this book, some of the names and faces at Headsets.com have changed. As I noted earlier in this book, several of the team have now moved on to establish Customer Service Excellence teams for premier companies across the United States.

While the names and faces may have changed a little, their Customer-centric philosophy powers on—adapting, evolving, and growing from strength to strength.

It is still my absolute pleasure to coach the Headsets.com teams in San Francisco and Nashville, and I even have the opportunity to work with some of the new teams established by former Customer Love experts. Which goes to show just how powerful the capital C can be.

I hope you've enjoyed and learned from this book. And I hope that I can experience some of your Customer Service Excellence firsthand one day. Look after your Customers. Make them a proper noun, and they'll make you famous (and maybe wealthy as well).

About the Author

Originally trained as a city planner, Ken Welsh soon diversified. First he specialized in transportation and became Australia's first local government transport planner, planning for Sydney City. Later he worked in numerous government agencies and private consultancies.

During his planning career, Ken was a rare entity—a working actor. He soon began directing and producing theater and television. After more than a decade, Ken continues as the artistic director of Australian-based Murder by Design, an interactive theater company specializing in team bonding.

The skills that he developed as a performer quickly led Ken into a new role in his planning career: stakeholder engagement and negotiation expert, working for numerous government agencies, corporations, and consultancies, including coordinating several working groups and advisory teams for the Sydney 2000 Olympics

Now, after more than twenty years of experience as a communicator, Ken has an unparalleled range of practical experience in communication, presentation, and negotiation. He is recognized internationally as a key proponent of the art of communication, and his clients include companies and executives in North America (United States, Canada, and Mexico),Europe and the United Kingdom, Africa, Asia, the Middle East, and Australia

Ken's specialty is the use of the psychological elements of language and their interface with emotions to create a unique experience for Customer Communication and business relationship management, or simply "getting your message across in the best possible way."

Ken's education includes

- a degree in town planning;
- a series of engineering certificates;
- diplomas in acting, drama, and performance;
- postgraduate studies in transport and traffic planning (not that anyone in their right mind would try to "plan" traffic);
- certificates in emotional intelligence, workplace creativity, and laughter work; and
- a PhD in behavioral psychology (examining the interface between language and behavior).

And, without sounding like a notice in a singles' magazine, Ken's likes, hobbies, and pastimes include

- loves travel, people, and cultures;
- prefers to be a traveler rather than a tourist;
- has a private pilot's license and a boat license;
- plays any sport that he can find time to;

- knows that
  - a trip is moving from A to B;
  - a journey is traveling from A to E via B, C, and D; and
  - An adventure is the series of serendipitous events that happen along the way.

Customer—with a Capital C

The Headsets.com Way to Customer-Centric Service

"This isn't just another book on Customer satisfaction. Ken Welsh provides an inside look into how Headsets.com grew significantly by putting their Customers first in every aspect of their business—and taking Customer Service to a whole new level. Ken's packed this book with real life examples, strategies, and actionable information that you and your business can put to work right away."

Michael Zipursky, cofounder of Advicetap.com

Ken Welsh has worked with over one hundred companies, their executives, and their teams, helping them deliver exemplary communication to all of their Customers—internal, external, and interpersonal. His diverse background includes a PhD in behavioral psychology, focusing on how language can create physiological change, which leads to behavioral change. Prior to his coaching career, Ken worked in government, private enterprise, city planning, television, airline, hospitality, tourism, and the entertainment industry, and he readily applies this broad range of experience to meeting the challenges of today's business world with innovative practical solutions.